Pure Permanent Make Up

101 + Secrets & Tricks

The difference between ordinary and extraordinary is practice

By

Inna

ISBN:

978-1-963764-74-1 (e-Book)
978-1-963764-72-7 (Paperback)
978-1-963764-73-4 (Hardback)

About the Author

Inna Argo is a highly respected permanent makeup artist with over a decade of experience in the beauty industry. With a passion for both the art and science of permanent makeup, Inna Argo has dedicated their career to helping others master the craft and achieve outstanding results for their clients.

I am a very open person, so feel free to contact me if you wish to know more or if you're interested in personal training with me.

WWW.PUREPERMANENTMAKEUP.COM

443-932-9137

IG@purepmu101

Preface

This information is for qualified permanent makeup PMU artists who feel that they require a better understanding of color theory. Although many cosmetic tattooing courses address this topic, the fundamentals of choosing appropriate pigments for certain skin types and ethnicities are often areas where training falls short. You simply cannot develop the depth of colorant knowledge required in a standard three to five-day foundation course. There are many elements to a successful tattoo application, including the quality of materials used, finesse of hand technique and stretch, and the ever-variable client skin type.

Add to these external influences such as climate, lighting in the treatment room, and visual acuity of the practitioner, making for a highly unpredictable healing outcome for the inexperienced. It isn't surprising that many cosmetic tattooists lack confidence when choosing pigments early on. When it comes to etching your work onto someone's face, this is an area where you don't want to gamble on your business livelihood. Skillful technicians are more capable, practice with confidence, and will operate a successful business in an environment where reputation is critical.

Introduction

There is not beauty without color, unknown.

The cosmetic tattooing industry has experienced a surge of interest in recent years, with demand driven by the focus on defined eyebrows and microblading. Social media has played a significant role in showcasing transformative before and after pictures of feathered eyebrows. Talented cosmetic tattooists have had their portfolios widely shared and made viral online. This has resulted in an influx of bookings and went viral online. This has resulted in an influx of bookings and spurred many in beauty and unrelated industries to train in the PMU field.

Although there are many great foundational cosmetic tattooing courses out there, they are largely focused on technique, drawing and hygiene or safety elements. For many new therapists, color theory is the most intimidating part of permanent makeup practice. Even after gaining their qualification, the ones often fall on the student to learn more about their topic in depth. This is done either through experience gained over time with clients or by investing in supplementary courses to leverage industry knowledge. While this may seem like a large expense (often ranging in the thousands for a few days), it is highly recommended that both new and practicing cosmetic tattooists commit to the investment.

Developing an understanding of color theory will only add value to your business, reduce the stress you experience in practice, and uphold the reputation of the PMU industry. It doesn't take much for one unhappy vocal client to discredit the cosmetic tattooing practice. This booklet aims to act as a reference guide for artists to further build on their knowledge. It by no means should be taken as a replacement for valuable practical training and ongoing core learning.

Contents

Why Is Color Theory So Important?

Simply put, it is to avoid the implantation of poor color choices. Choosing the wrong pigment mix for your client can result in an unattractive result against their skin tone, dreaded blue or red faded tattoos, or a grey and ashen healed outcome. Even if the client is happy with the shape or hair strokes that you have applied, the resultant color can ruin what was otherwise a well-done procedure.

Inexperienced technicians determine their color selection by matching pigment shades to the client's current coloring. They will swab a sample of the pigment against the client's current coloring. They will swab a sample of the pigment against the client's forehead and pick a shade that closely resembles existing hair. Although this is a common practice, which is also done by highly skilled PMU artists, the difference is that this swab needs to be considered in line with how it will merge with the skin undertone, not just a face value. This oversimplifies the dynamics of implanting pigment that will be incorporated into the skin upon healing. Rarely will you encounter a client who is a neutral and blank canvas- that is, what you see in the bottle is what you get in a healed result.

Be wary that some pigment bottles are also slightly opaque to preserve the contents. A seemingly dark brown shade can be masked and appear lighter upon application. PMU artists need training in their chosen pigment line so that they understand the dominant hue of each shade.

The Principles of Color Theory

Traditional color theory imparts a reference point for technicians to use when understanding how combining colors will produce desired client results. This knowledge is critical to your success as a PMU artist, yet it is an area where many lack extensive training.

Color is the visual by-product of the spectrum of light as it is either transmitted through a transparent medium or as it is absorbed and reflected off a surface. Color is the light wavelengths that the human eye receives and processes from reflected sources. When referring to color, it is determined visually by measurement of the following:

Hue

The dominant wavelength of visible color is what is readily experienced that we see, e.g., yellow.

Saturation

The strength and intensity of a color, e.g., dull or bright.

Value

The quality of light reflected, the lightness or darkness of a color, e.g., tint, pastel or rich.

Primary, Secondary and Tertiary Colors

The *primary* colors are *red*, *yellow* and blue. They are the only colors that cannot be made by mixing any other colors. *Secondary* colors are mixtures of two primary colors. Color theory denotes that equal proportions of primaries are formed by the relationship between lightness and density. Understanding the strength ratio between primary colors will help to determine pigment mixtures for color corrections.

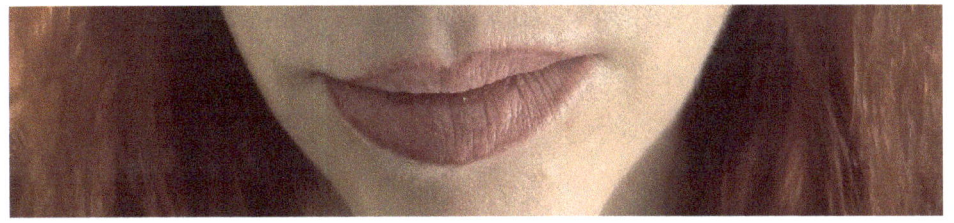

Before

My client had a dark blue outline on her lips, and she didn't want it.
I Used a yellow corrector to remove that color.

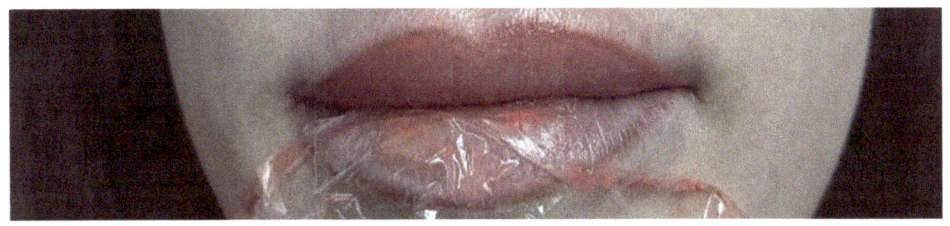

Working process

Upper lip done. Doesn't it look beautiful?

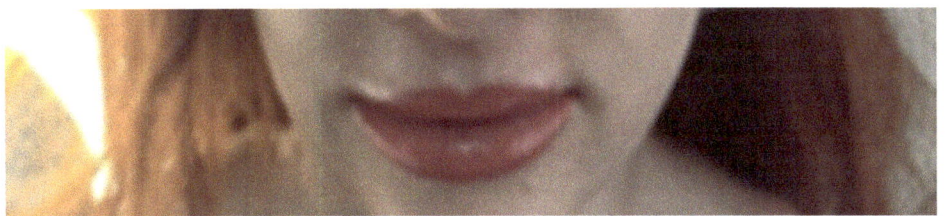

After

Happy client with no blue line

Yellow is the lightest and requires two times as much to equal the destiny of red and three times as much to equal the destiny of blue.

Red requires two portions to meet the destiny of blue (blue is not used as a corrective modifier color due to this high density and its tendency to heal the darkest in the skin). For example, Orange is formed from a combination of three parts: yellow and two parts red.

Tertiary or intermediate colors are a mixture of one primary and one secondary color. Most cosmetic tattooing pigments are a result of tertiary mixtures, e.g., brown.

While it is useful to understand traditional color theory, the complicated factor for PMU artists is that it is overly simplistic for our purposes. To grasp color theory as it applies to cosmetic tattooing is to appreciate the application of color contained in pigment to the colored skin of our clients. A skilled technician must understand the base color of each pigment used and how this will interact with their canvas- the client's face and incorporate this knowledge to produce the desired result.

Blue + **Yellow** = **Green**

Yellow + **Red** = Orange

Blue + **Red** = Purple

Yellow + Purple = Brown

Orange + **Blue** = Brown

Yellow + **Red** = Brown

Warm Versus Cool Colors

Colors fall into two main categories, often defined as the relative temperature of a hue, being either warm or cool. The classification of the primary colors is below:

- *Blue-Cool*

- *Yellow- Both warm and Cool*

- *Red- Warm*

Warm Colors - Red, yellow, and orange

These Colors evoke warmth because they remind us of things like the sun.

Cool Colors - Blue, green, purple (violet)

These colors evoke a cool feeling because they remind us of things like water or grass.

Neutral Colors - Gray and brown

These aren't on most color wheels, but they're considered neutral because they don't contrast with much of anything.

Pigment Ingredient Basics

Pigments are the soul of permanent Makeup!

The tattoo inks used in permanent makeup comprise two primary parts; colorant or pigment particles and a form of liquid carrier that facilitates the delivery of the pigment into the skin. They are detailed further below:

Colorants + Liquid Carrier = Pigment Bottle

Colorants

Colorants impart color to the ink and are the major components of the pigment formulation. Tattoo colorants are typically pigments that are held in place by intermolecular or physical forces, being weakly attracted to one another. These intensely colored compounds reflect light in the visible region of the light spectrum.

Historically, pigments used in tattoo inks were derived from geological or mineral sources to produce colors and hues. More recently, manufacturers have moved away from mineral-based, and approximately 60 percent of these organic pigments are azon pigments. Pigments are ground into a very fine powder and then added to a binder to create the final bottled formula. Components of a pigment powder commonly include:

Inorganic

- Iron oxides

- Titanium Dioxide

- Manganese Violet

- Ultramarines

Organic

- Azon

- Dyes

- Lakes

- Carbon

Organic Pigments

Inorganic Pigments

Organic ink is made of fruit or vegetable-based pigments, also called "lake pigments. They are oil dispensable, which just means the color dye will blend in with your skin more naturally with little to no clumping.

Organic pigments impart a very rich color to the brows and will have a brighter color effect as opposed to a dull, faded look. Using organic pigments gives you that your brow color will not change, or fight with your skin tone.

However, exposure to sunlight or chemicals can take away the bright color of organic pigments.

Inorganic ink consists of the main ingredient is often found in association with other metal-containing acids such as lead, arsenic, and mercury.

Inorganic ink also contains preservatives, perfumes, and other additives, so when the ink is applied to the skin it has the risk of causing a severe reaction and sometimes even permanent damage if not applied correctly.

Iron oxides are lightweight as compared to organic pigments. They are less intense in color than certified organic colors. Zinc oxide and iron oxide help with opacity, meaning that they provide a solid color that is not transparent. But, because of the high iron content color of eyebrows changes over time.

Pigments with smaller particle sizes will last longer in the skin compared to pigments with larger particle sizes.

Yellow has large particle sizes. Therefore, yellow usually fades first.

Red has small particle sizes. Therefore, red lasts very long in the skin.

Liquid Carriers

Tattoo Inks contain liquid carriers whose primary function is to allow colorant molecules to enter the skin. They hold the whole substance together, add moisture, and quite often also contain solvents that allow the production of pigment. Another function of these additives is to keep the pigments in uniform suspension to avoid microorganism growth in the product after opening.

After the pigment has been implanted into the dermal layer of the skin, the suspended solution evaporates, and the oxides revert to dried particles upon healing.

Common liquid carriers include:

- Aqua, distilled or purified water
- Isopropyl alcohol
- Rosin
- Isopropyl palmitate
- Witch hazel propylene glycol
- Glycerin

Organic and Inorganic Pigments- Misconceptions

In the modern beauty industry, the term "organic" generally refers to plant-based or naturally occurring ingredients. These products are made without the use of CMOs, pesticides, herbicides, or parabens and often come with an organic certification. In the permanent makeup industry, the term organic does not refer to products of a natural origin or those that are devoid of nasty chemicals. Organic pigments are not superior pigments and are not intended to refer to health and well-being. Rather, the definition is more science-based, with all cosmetic tattoo pigments being produced synthetically in labs. These pigments are often composed of organic or inorganic colorant compounds or a mixture of both. A general breakdown of the differences is detailed below:

Inorganic Pigments

- Not Comprised of carbon (the backbone of living organisms)

- Duller, more earthy, muted color tones

- Formed from metal complexes, e.g., from oxides, ultramarines, titanium dioxide, and chromium oxide.

- Harder to break down with high stability and high particle dispersion.

- Titanium dioxide (white) is often added to lighten the pigment color.

- Larger particle size compared to organic pigments.

- Organic Pigments

- Contains carbon and hydrogen molecules within the chemical structure.

- Includes some lakes (metal salts), azon dyes and other compounds.

- Brighter and more vibrant colors, but with limited variety

- Do not last as long as inorganic pigments.

- Man-made and synthesized from chemical formulations.

- Nothing to do with agricultural references.

- Expensive and not environmentally sustainable to produce.

- Higher risk of carrying bacteria, which can cause adverse health reactions or allergies compared to inorganic colorants.

Difference between Cosmetic Tattoo and Body Art Tattoo Pigments

Cosmetic tattoo pigments are very different from body art links, both in terms of result and composition. Pigments used in the PMU field are often referred to as semi-permanent and are designed to gradually fade over time due to skin type, environmental or lifestyle factors, and depending on the depth of implantation in the skin (the shallower, the faster the degree of fading). Comprised of largely inorganic colorants such as cosmetic-grade iron oxides and lakes, these inks are softer, more muted hues in natural tones that are formed from tertiary colors.

In contrast, body art pigments are formed from bright primary and secondary colors and are typically permanent in nature due to the presence of carbon. Traditional tattoo inks are bolder and more vivid from higher levels of organic colorant in the mixtures. While they are designed to last, fading can occur with sun exposure and after with skin changes over time.

A common question from clients relates to why PMU artists do not use body art pigments for cosmetic purposes, and theoretically, this would mean fewer touch-ups and less maintenance. Purely from an aesthetic point of view, the use of muted colors produces a much more natural result that can mimic existing brow hairs or lip shading. An effective result enhances current features rather than overwhelming a face. Permanent makeup that initially appears flattering may later clash with changing skin tones and facial contours. As a person ages, clients will also be able to change pigment color or adjust a faded tattoo shape that corrects for drooping or aging of the skin, e.g., lifting eyebrows to get a brighter-eyed look.

Impact of Pigment Particle Size

Further to differences in composition, the particle size of cosmetic tattoo pigments compared to body art pigments also vary. The way in which this affects the healed result is best understood in the context of the client's immune response; when a needle is used to implant ink into the dermis, this creates a wound that causes the body to send specialized cells to the site of damage.

These "defense" cells, called fibroblasts and macrophages, work to swallow foreign bodies and absorb the tattoo ink. Body art pigments are comprised of particles that are too large for the defense cells to destroy, so they remain implanted in the dermis.

In contrast, cosmetic tattoo pigments contain smaller particles that are more readily absorbed by immune cells. This causes the implanted color to fade and metabolize at a faster rate, requiring a greater frequency of top-up treatments. There is a greater risk of pigment migration (spread into areas outside of the implantation site) if colorant particle sizes are too small.

If PMU pigment molecules were larger, the color would be denser and more permanent in nature. Note that relative particle size also has an impact on the success of laser removal procedures in a similar manner, being that body art pigments are more difficult to fragment and absorb compared to cosmetic tattoo inks. A body art tattoo is likely to require more laser sessions to produce a satisfactory outcome for clients.

Picking a Pigment Line

Apart from salon rent, pigments are likely to be the most expensive operating cost of your business. These consumables are from the base of a technician's toolkit, and you must find a reputable brand. Most tattooists continue to use the same pigment line that was provided in their fundamental training. Often, these brands are lower in quality as it is more financially viable for training. Often, these brands are lower in quality as it is more financially viable for training institutions. New pigment brands, some with grandiose product claims, are hitting the market all the time, and PMU artists need to decipher between the good and bad lines. The following are key indicators and questions to look for when picking a manufacturer:

Word of Mouth

Speak to experienced peers in the industry or join one of the credible cosmetic tattooing Facebook groups online – the quality groups usually screen for member qualifications before approval. There will be an abundance of information on recommended pigment lines if you do a post-search. Once you find a manufacturer that you trust, start with a simple palate of colors and do not use a combination of brands. Note that the names given to pigment colors across brands are not standardized if you encounter similar titles.

PMU "Influencers"

Many well-known trainers in the PMU field release their own line of pigments to supplement their course offerings. Often, these brands are touted as the best fit for a technique (e.g., micro-blading) or work well with certain blades or needles. While some of these lines are high quality, others are private label average pigments where you are paying a premium for branding. Ensure you invest in quality, not fluff.

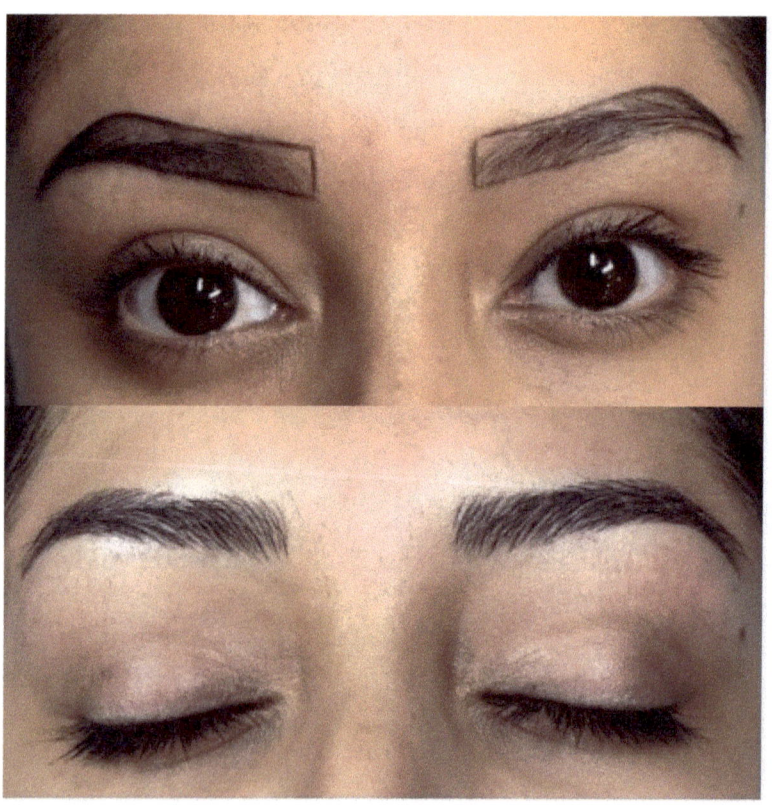

Brand Longevity

As you know, healed tattoo results can vary over time. Sometimes, these results are unexpected and are due to low-quality pigments rather than technician error. Many new brands have come and gone, but some reputable lines have been industry favorites for decades. PMU artists can reliably predict how a tattoo will heal once they have grasped the color theory and application of a pigment brand. Stick to the industry leaders with stable color performance over time.

Manufacturer Disclosure

Manufacturers are not required to reveal the contents of their pigments as the information is proprietary. The U.S. Food and Drug Administration (FDA) does not regulate inks that are placed under the skin. Given the wide-ranging allergies and adverse reactions that clients could exhibit or disclose on your forms, it is essential to pick a brand that provides a comprehensive ingredient list. Note that with "fakes," you are unlikely to get any information or possibly false ingredient labels.

Materials Safety Data Sheets (MSDS)

The larger, more reputable pigment manufacturers will provide Material Safety Data Sheets with their products – usually one sheet per pigment color. Their reference document contains useful information about handling and safety precautions, pigment toxicity, PH, and emergency advice. They often also supply product identifiers, color swatches, ingredient composition (if not provided separately), storage and waste treatment guidelines, and some have conducted allergy testing and disclosed results. As a cosmetic tattooist, you should familiarize yourself with the MSDS to ensure that you have a working understanding of the pigment line.

Light fastness Rating

Lightfastness refers to the chemical stability or resistance of a pigment to change when exposed to UV light over time. As an energy source, light can cause color and chemical changes in many pigments. In permanent makeup, controlling for other individual factors, knowing the lightfastness rating would help to determine the longevity or stability of a tattoo. The most common industry scales are the Blue Wool Scale (1 being very poor to 8 being excellent lightfastness with low fading) and the American Standard Test Measure (ASTM), which benchmarks between 1 to V in descending order of excellent to poor color retention. When manufacturers combine colorants in a pigment mix, they need to ensure that the lightfast ratings of each component are similar.

Suppose the lightfast properties of each colorant are not balanced. In that case, they will degrade at different rates, leaving behind a dominant, often undesirable hue in the tattoo that is different from the original pigment color. Ensure that you select a pigment line with optimized lightfastness to avoid unexpected changes. For most reputable brands, this means a 7-8 Blue Wool Rating or I ASTM scale. Your results should not fade to different colors, only lighter versions of the original color. In practice, this rating is not widely disclosed by pigment companies, and you will need to contact them directly for further information. Some brands will also reference their approach to product lightfastness on their website's frequently asked questions page.

Pigment Load

This refers to the amount of pigment compared to the amount of binder and carrier ingredients in each bottle. Quality brands tend to have a higher pigment load, resulting in a more concentrated hue and a lower propensity for color change and fading. These brands can be pricier, which reflects the cost of materials. Cosmetic tattooists can manipulate the pigment load to achieve desired client outcomes by using a supplementary dilution solution (usually sold alongside the main pigment line and comprising of alcohol, distilled water and glycerin). A 100 percent pigment mix can be diluted down to 75 percent to achieve that powdery eyebrow or soft, smoky eyeliner look. Ensure that you utilize a brand's dilution scale or guidelines before attempting to modify a mixture.

Color identification charts

CIC mini brands provide color identification charts for tattooists to use and quickly refer to during treatment. These posters or booklets detail the color index of each pigment color temperature (cool-neutral-warm), the base tone of each color in the line recommended color for each skin, tone type, corrective colors to use, and gradient swatches. Once you have a master or pigment line chart won't be as necessary, but for the novice PMU artists, the CIC plan can be unavailable to gain confidence in pigment choices.

Pigment skin testing.

This refers to the process in which game PMU artists test for clients, allergies or sensitivities to pigment. To an extent, this test can mitigate the risk of making poor color choices as it can be used to assess healed outcomes. A patch test, whereby a small quantity of the pigment intended for use in the tattoo procedure is inserted in the most widely used technique to do this. The client then waits a few weeks until the pigment has healed before they start their request for a procedure. This is not a guarantee but a good indication if a person will have any type of reaction to the products. Although this method is used by many professionals in the field, there are some problems with the approach to note:

Pigments may only react on some areas of the body and not others. Different areas can be healed. Outcomes due to the environment body (e.g., certain body parts experience more sun explodes, which can impact the result) and structural factors, such as varying skill thickness on the forehead compared to the neck.

The timeframe between testing and healing may be insufficient. Actual healing can take between six weeks to three months to see a stable result. Most treatments occur within a week of the patch test. Allergic reactions can occur months and even years after the fact.

The quantity of pigments used can change the outcome. Small patch tests use negligible amounts, and the body may be non-reactive in these instances. However, clients who are exposed to the same pigment at a high level during a procedure can react adversely.

If you are opting to undertake scheme texting, ensure that the client is well briefed on the risks and limitations. Aim to use the patch on the same area as the treatment itself and use more than a minute amount. Try to allow a minimum timeframe for healing starting from four weeks, which aligns with the skin regeneration cycle. Also, ensure that you have comprehensive client medical history forms to gain a broad understanding of risks and contraindications. Clients with a history of allergy-related eczema, psoriasis or other skin or other skin conditions are at higher risk of complications as tattoos can sometimes exacerbate the symptoms. People with sensitivities to jewelry, hair, dyes, or beauty products. I am not a subgroup to be wary of. This is due to the presence of iron oxides in many pigments and their widespread use in this cosmetic product.

Tattoo Healing And Coloring Change

It would be safe to say that every PMU artist receives their fair share of concerned texts or calls from clients during the healing phase. Queries ranging from "the pigment has disappeared" to "the color is completely different" are not unusual in nature. As a skilled technician, you need to understand and be able to articulate with a client perceives to reassure them.

This is best explained through the process of pigment fixation, whereby the tattoo will vary in color as the body's immune cells fixate and surround the foreign pigment, trying to remove it. In response to the tattooing procedure, any trauma or wound to the skin will be repaired in the part of the migration of keratinocyte cells to form a hardened barrier or scabbing. This barrier serves to protect the new tattoo from external damage, such as UV light, bacteria, and various environmental elements.

As the tattoo heels during the skin keratinization cycle (replenishment of dead skin cells over two to four weeks), the implanted pigment will change in appearance. Below is a general outline of the expected healing process and its impact on color:

Week one

A pigment became fixated on the skin. The color initially appears quite bold due to excess pigments in the epidermis. The tattooed area might be swollen and patchy due to the swelling and clusters of immune cells rushing to the site of trauma. Clients may be worried that the stage the tattoo artist later than usual drawings you do is temporary Inflammation.

Week two

Any swelling or redness should have subsided by now, and the boldness of the tattoo will be reduced by up to 60%. This is due to the pigment in the epididymis flaking and shedding off during regeneration. The client may be concerned that their tattoo is too faded and light at this point; pigment implanted in the skin dermal cells can be masked by the dead top of the layer of the skin while new skin forms beneath.

Week three

The pigment color should begin to return in boldness. This occurs as the concentration of immune cells around the tattoo reduces in number, and macrophage and connective fibroblast cells become permanently suspended in the dermis. These cells have absorbed the pigment, and the color in the cells shows through the skin.

Week four to six

The tattoo will be in the last stage of healing, and the final color will be evident, inclusive of natural skin tone color influences. Note that the tattoo may look slightly cloudy for food in a few weeks. This is because the upper skin layer has healed, but the deeper layers of the skin repair at a slower rate, so clients will need to continue care of their tattoos.

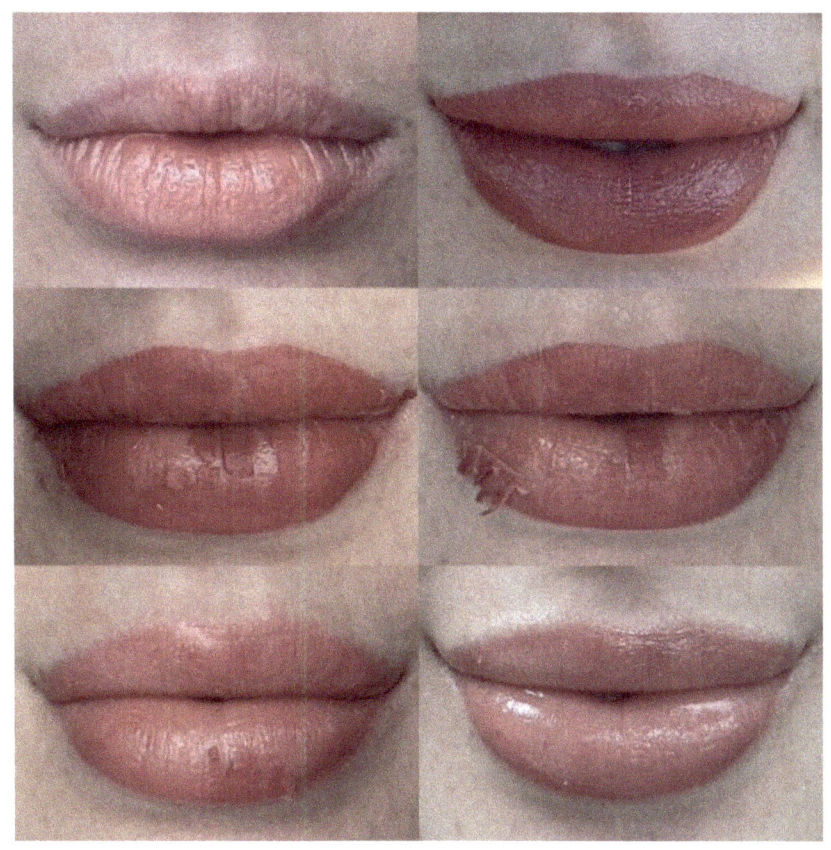

The above process may be prolonged in the timeframe when applied to an appendage area. The human face is quite vascular and metabolizes pigment at a faster rate than body-app appendages such as an arm or leg. This is one of the reasons why a facial tattoo will fade pigment much faster than traditional body art. Commonly absorbed in the eyebrow. Tattoos have the tendency to the tail and tend to retain pigment longer if there is little movement in that region. The front bulb area tends to fade faster due to the high level of movement by eyebrow musculature.

Why do cosmetic tattoos change color?

There is a range of causes that can be attributed to unexpected changes in tattoo color. Experienced PMU artist knows how to diagnose the reason behind the anomalies and exercise good judgment when taking action to correct them. The following among the most common causes to consider:

Client skin undertone

Melanin levels in the skin can add color to the final healed outcome of the tattoo if not corrected for by the tattooist.

Medication and medical conditions

There may be conditions that react with the pigment molecules. For example, clients taking acne medication such as Accutane can have hypersensitive skin that doesn't retain color and is prone to scarring.

Those taking blood thinners such as aspirin are also at risk of pigment bleeding out during the tattooing process, as well as poor clotting.

Skincare, products, and treatments used by the client

Harsh chemicals, such as alpha hydroxyl of retinoid, can cause fading. More aggressive salon treatments such as laser, dermabrasion and chemical peels can also affect the color of a cosmetic tattoo. Another understood cause of color change is the tendency of some over clean their face; removal of dirt and oils is healthy, but excessive cleansing will dry out the skin, disrupting the hydration barrier and irritating the tattoo.

Sun explosion or internal environment factors

Clients exposed to high ultraviolet radiation UV of those who work outdoors may observe a change in vibrancy along with fading in the sharpness or detail of their tattoos. Even some indoor lighting sources, such as fluorescent and halogen bulbs, can emit significant levels of UV, which penetrate through the skin.

Alcohol consumption

Like the impact of blood thinning medications, alcohol has an anticoagulant effect on blood clotting, which can cause the client to bleed more than usual post-treatment. Clients who are regular drinkers should abstain from alcohol for two days prior to their appointment to increase the chance of pigment retention.

Smoking

Cigarettes can have multiple inboxes on the tattoo from a hundred wounds, healing excessive bleeding, leading to pigment migration during the treatment and reducing collagen production, which affects skin quality and elasticity.

Skins cellular composition

Clients with high concentrations of sebaceous glands (oily skin types) in their dermal layer can take up color differently, often requiring more touch-ups. The use of water-based pigment as opposed to a glycerin-based product may help to prevent color lifting onto the skin surface.

Failure to adhere to aftercare instructions.

If the client picked the scab, washed the wound too soon, or went to the pool or sauna before the tattoo was fully healed.

Quality of pigment used.

How fresh the pigment was, whether the pigment was properly stored, and the source of composition of powders used in the production all impact color.

Tattoo method.

Whether pigment was implanted correctly into the upper reticular, dermal skin layer and not too deep (or else color will run cooler for or blue out) and if the stretching technique to sneak was correct. A pigment that is incorrectly applied to the epidermal layer will not be permanent and will shed during the skin healing cycle.

Needle configuration.

The smaller the needle configuration, the cooler and more Orange the color may appear.

Client skin tone

PMU artists often encounter conflicting information about Color theory relative to skin tone when they seek to expand their knowledge. Many resources detailing traditional color concepts in the beauty industry have been assimilated from other training programs, namely in the makeup application field. The lens you need to apply in a cosmetic tattooing framework is unique, as the skin tone will heal and blend with your pigment over time. This is markedly more complex than applying a flattering lip or shadow color on top of the skin.

What makes cosmetics tattooing particularly challenging is the fact that every face form is a unique canvas, with its own skin composition along with skin tones that can vary across the seasons. PMU artists need to have a good understanding of different complexions and incorporate this into their technique. A client's complexion is affected by many factors- genetic makeup, nutrition, environmental factors, and even disease conditions (albinism or vitiligo) can play a role in the color of skin.

One of the most notable components of the skin that contributes to the complexion is a big pigment known as Melanin. This pigment largely determines skin color and is present in different forms and ratios. It is also the pigment responsible for determining hair and eye color. Melanin is produced in specialized cells called melanocytes that do not behave the same way for all people. Some people naturally produce less Melanin, which can mean less pigment in the lighter skin.

Conversely, those with a higher level of Melanin will generally exhibit darker skin. People can also temporarily change the color of their skin by tanning, which stimulates the production of Melanin and inflames the area to protect against excessive UV explosives. This is why PMU artists need to take environmental and seasonal factors into consideration during pigment selection.

Further to this, it is important to note that the person's skin tone and undertone are not the same thing. Skin outer tone can change over time, but undertones remain constant. As the name suggests, undertones are the colors beneath the surface of the skin rather than what we observe at face value. Understanding your client's outer and undertones will mean the difference between a successful cosmetic tattooing outcome and one that has a poor aesthetic result.

Skin outer tone

Human skin comes in a wide variety of colors, ranging from shades of dark brown to almost white. There are no people who have true white, black, red or yellow skin, as Melanin within the epidermis will add these hues to the cells. While the focus of traditional color analysis is on determining the more obscure undertone, it is the Melanin in the outer tone that'll have the most influence on the outcome. A client's outer tone will add color to the healed result of any tattoo from above the implanted pigment.

Skin Undertone

An undertone is the color from beneath the surface of your skin that affects your overall hue.

The amount of Melanin in the dermal layer determines the undertone. The less Melanin a client has, the more their veins will show a hue and the cooler the complexion they will have. Those with more Melanin have veins that appear green and the warmer their complexion. The influence of the undertone on the client's healed result will depend on the saturation level of the implant pigment. The three main classifications of skin undertone are:

Warm:

if the base tone of the skin skews to green peach, sallow, yellow or gold.

Cool

if you see hints of blue, pink or red (ruddy complexion).

Neutral

if there is a mixture of both warm and cool hues with no obvious choice or if the undertone is roughly the same color as the actual skin tone.

Note that clients can also fall somewhere in between, such as *neutral warm*. For instance, some people with olive complexion have ashen or grey undertones. There is no obvious categorization, but isn't that a combination of undertones? It is also possible to have the same skin outer tone as someone else but have a completely different undertone. Accordingly, another misconception concerning undertone is that fairer clients can't have warm undertones, or dark-skinned clients can't have cool tones. This could be further from the truth. This is why it is important to determine true undertones rather than generalize by ethnicity, as in the common beginner practice.

The Fitzpatrick Scale

The handy tool for classifying your client's skin type and tone is known as the Fitzpatrick Scale, originally developed in 1975, which is used to access skin care using a numerical scale that measures the amount of melanin in the skin after exposure to the sun. The scale uses physical features to determine skin tone, eye color, and natural hair color. Most recently, it has been used by practitioners to determine suitability for laser and beauty treatments.

The Fitzpatrick Skin Types

Type 01

Extremely fair skin, always burns, never tans.

Type 02

Fair skin, always burns, sometimes tans

Type 03

Medium skin, sometimes
burns, always tans

Type 04

Moderately pigmented brown
skin, never burns, always tans

Type 05

Olive skin rarely burns, always tans.

Type 06

Markedly pigmented black skin, never burns, always tans

Many easy-to-use free online questionnaires determine Fitzpatrick skin type. Some cosmetic tattooists add these questions to their consent forms to ensure that they have a good understanding of their client's skin tendencies and type prior to treatment.

In practice, PMU technicians can use the scale to determine the level of saturation of melanin in the skin. Understanding the extent to which natural skin color influences the healing result of the tattoo will inform your pigment choice. For example, clients assessed as Type I Fitzpatrick will typically produce lower levels of melanin, inferring a typically cool undertone. This means that the pigment will show well, and you need to adjust your mixture accordingly with warning modifiers.

Conversely, clients with Type IV or V of Fitzpatrick-type skin typically have higher concentrations of melanin and skew towards warmer undertones. Note that this scale should only be taken as a reference point, and you will need to make more individualized assessments to ensure the right color choice is made (for example, the vein test to work out the dominant hue, et cetera).

Another use for the Fitzpatrick scale in cosmetic tattooing is knowing the client's susceptibility to post-inflammatory hyperpigmentation (PIH). Those who are assessed as Fitzpatrick Type IV to VI are particularly prone to PIH. Clients who have or may develop PIH have hyperactive melanocyte cells, and if their skin experiences any form of irritation, their melanocyte cells may be stimulated to produce more melanin. This can result in unsightly darkened spots or discoloration that can obscure the actual tattoo pigment or cause it to look patchy.

Be wary that this masking of the tattoo can often be misconstrued by clients as a change in the pigment color rather than an inflammatory skin reaction. Should you choose to take on higher PIH risk clients, it is recommended that you explain the potential for adverse reactions for the individual, ask that they seek medical advice if there are existing darkened blemishes which may be PIH (could be from previous irritation, such acne or rashes), and undertake a small patch test at least a month before the treatment so you can check for sign of discoloration.

Identifying Your Client's Skin Tone

While the Fitzpatrick scale can be useful for understanding skin types and tendencies, cosmetic tattooists need to be mindful that this is a guideline of melanin saturation and not an absolute measure of skin hue. Further analysis of your client's true skin tone is recommended to ensure the best aesthetic results and understand how skin will react.

A basic PMU rule to remember is:

Pigment + skin tone + healing over time

=

final tattoo result after exfoliation

This is why it's so critical to understand each component of your equation and control for the factors that you can. The following methods can help you determine the dominant skin tone, noting that each reference point should not be considered isolation. However, when coupled with other tests, it can help narrow down options and determine the right tone:

You will find in the practice that most clients have cool undertones, and skin becomes cooler with age. Sun damage can also influence skin towards coolness, so take the climate of your area into account.

The Face Test

Ask your clients to arrive at their appointment with no makeup on or use a wipe to remove any base foundation completely. Start by looking at your client's clean face in the natural light. Pay attention to the corners of their mouth and sides of the nose, as this is where the undertone is most evident. If they have peachy yellow golden pigments, they are likely warm toned. If pink, reds, or blues are visible, they're probably cool-toned. If they have a mix of colors, or you can tell, they're likely neutral. Remember, when you're viewing your color, you are viewing it through your client's skin. If you are still struggling to determine the undertone, place a sheet of white paper next to the client. This will help your eyes discern and contrast better as the white acts as a baseline neutral canvas.

The Vein Test

Attempt to look through your client's skin as the inner part of their arm and the veins on the inside of the wrist. The color of their veins will help you determine the undertone. If the veins appear to be green, this indicates a warm undertone. If they are bluish and purple in color, then you are likely dealing with cool undertones.

The Eye Test

Clients who have golden brown green or hazel eyes with gold flex are likely to be warm. This is often validated if they also have strawberry blonde, auburn or black hair with gold tones. Clients with hazel or blue eyes with grey flecks are more likely to be cool toned. They also tend to have blonde, brown, or black hair with platinum tones. Ensure that you check for enhancements such as contact lenses and hair dye.

The Jewelry Test

Jewelry is another way to determine what someone's undertone is. Ask your client what the usual blue preference is in terms of gold or silver variations. If they tend to adore gold accessories, this is generally best suited to those with a warm undertone. If silver is more flattering on your client, the undertones are cool. If both gold and silver look good on a person, then they might have neutral undertones.

The Sun Test

Ask your client about how their skin tends to react when exposed to the sun. If they tend to burn or pink in the sunlight, then they are cool toned. If your client mainly tans when they go out in the sun, they're warm-toned. Note that some individuals will fall in the middle, and this measure can be quite subjective (for instance, the client may, in fact, burn, but they do so after a period).

General Guide

Client Feature	Skin Tone	Extra Considerations
Green Veins with a tendency to tan	*Warm undertone*	Gold jewelry looks best on this skin type
Blue or purple veins, burn easily and tan a little	*Cool Undertone*	Silver jewelry looks best on this skin type
Mix of Blue and green veins with Olive Skin	*Neutral undertone*	The true hair color of those with olive skin is often darker brown
Fair or porcelain appearance that freckles or burns easily, usually with violet around the eyes (transparent skin)	*Cool undertone*	Can have quite sensitive skin and react to any inflammation.

Ivory porcelain skin with blue influence around the eyes. The client's lips will often appear pink purple in color (translucent skin).	*Neutral to cool undertone*	These clients mainly burn and tan minimally, if at all. Cool-based pigments will usually ash out to grey on this client.
Sallow yellow skin type, commonly of Asian ethnicity.	*Neutral to cool undertone*	Tends to pull darker upon healing if yellow keratin is present
Darker skin type – like African or Indian ethnicity	*Warm undertone*	Prone to post-inflammatory hyperpigmentation.

Use of Pigment Modifiers

In the ideal world, all clients would have completely neutral skin tones in their tattoos, which would heal as applied. Given that this is an unlikely scenario, we need to leverage color theory principles and pigment modifiers in practice.

Modifiers are a range of corrective pigments, available alongside primary pigment offerings, that are produced by manufacturers to serve two main functions:

1) assist with color corrections

2) to modify colors as needed

For example, to darken an existing brown pigment and avoid having to purchase multiple brown shades—this enables you to work with the limited range and ensure fresher pigments with a better product turnover. Modifier pigments are highly concentrated green, yellow and orange shades and should be used sparingly. Blue must have quite a density to be used as a modifier, twice as strong as red and three times the density of Yellow. Orange is also used in lieu of Red, as red can have transparent properties and a poor ability to mask unwanted skin tones.

The following are key principles to note when using modifiers:

1. As a basic rule, cool colors neutralize warm colors and vice versa.

2. Complementary colors correct or neutralize because they absorb light from colors.

3. Almost all pigments will heal in the skin cooler than they appear on the surface. It is generally better to add warmth to the mixture. If a client returns too warm, then you can either leave out the warmer pigment or add a cool one upon touch-up. If you have used a cool mixture incorrectly, then the client can heal grey, and this becomes more difficult to deal with as it is now a correction.

4. A pigment will stay true to its dominant hue even when a modifier is added as long as you use a small and prescribed amount as per the brand guidelines. The client's skin tone will absorb the modifier in line with its color collective function.

5. Avoiding eyebrows in big months does have a blue basin discolor. It's to dance, and it's getting the result in my violet eyebrows.

When using modifiers to change your base pigment, use the color complement (opposing color on the color wheel) to darken a pigment. Ensure that you don't add too much, as modifiers are very strong.

In general:

- Orange is a complementary color to Blue-Grey and Green.

- Yellow is a complementary color to Violet.

- Green is a complementary color to Orange and Red.

For example, if you want to use cooler brown, you will add a small amount of green modifier to the neutral brown color. If you want a warmer brown, you add a small amount of Orange or ochre modifier.

When using modifiers to make color corrections, remember that red, blue, and violet are not used as the correct colors.

Always attempt to fix the color as a priority; one considers shape if the client requests an update.

Ensure you know the base color of a pigment, as this is critical when attempting to make a correction. A color modification chart should be provided with all the brands.

Most corrections will require multiple appointments for the corrective color to blend with the original tattoo during healing. For example, a tattoo that has faded to blue will take at least two sessions to influence color change. Make sure you manage expectations with clients in advance, given the cost and time implications.

Remember that colors fade to different shades, from darker to medium and light. When adding modifiers generally for dark shades, you can use the correction color undiluted on the tattoo. Medium shades require at least five drops of dilution solution or desired pigment to one drop of modifier. For lighter shades, choose the desired colors, then add a few drops of the correction collar until neutralized.

As mentioned above, if the unwanted pigment is not too dense, then you may want to apply the boss of straight modifier first, then follow with a blend of target color plus corrector. The client may be concerned about their unsightly green or orange tattoo, so you will need to reassure them that this is the correct one as it heals. Each step can be completed across multiple appointments if you prefer to see the healed results between passes.

Depending on what outcome the clients want and the saturation level of their unwanted color, the tattoo may require laser removal followed by correction. If the original pigment is too dense, then the correction will not last.

Pigment in scar tissue will become more resistant to taking up color over cumulative treatments. This means that it will be harder to implant pigment and tattoo a client over time, and you will need to consider turning away their business and refresh, and it won't last long.

The clients need to be advised that their color will fade over time. If not refreshed every few years, then it will fade and leave a residue in the skin.

Healed Result	Corrective Color to Use
Blue	Orange or Yellow
Green	Red-based Browns or Mahogany
Red	Green or Olive
Pink	Light Green or Yellow

Violet	Yellow or Light Orange
Dark Grey	Orange or Rust
Yellow	Brown with Minimal Yellow
Orange	Green or Olive

Using the Color Wheel

The easiest visual representation of color theory principles is the color wheel, a circular configuration of the whole color spectrum. It starts with primary colors and moves out to secondary and tertiary colors. Cool colors (blue and green region) are located on the side of warm colors (red and yellow region) are on their opposite. The basic premise is that any two colors of opposite sides and equal spacing on the wheel will be complementary and work well together. This is because opposite colors are able to neutralize or correct each other as they absorb light.

Most complementary pairs are composed of the primary and one secondary color.

Cosmetic tattoo artists use the color wheel alongside their knowledge of skin tones and modifiers to choose the correct pigment blend. Corrective colors like Green, Yellow, and Orange are commonly used in permanent makeup to counteract unexpected results.

Picking a Pigment Mixture

Selecting a pigment mix for your client with confidence is a critical part of your entrusted role as a cosmetic tattoo. This is by no means an exact science, but understanding factors that influence color change will help to achieve the best results. Suppose you have picked a reputable pigment brand. In that case, the manufacturer will provide a color and identification chart along with MGMS documents to uniform your mixture and selection process. Use these guidelines along with below to determine color choice:

- **Number 1**- Ask your client what their preference Is in terms of desired color (dark brown or blonde) and saturation (light and more natural appearance or intense like makeup).

- **Number 2**- Consider your client's existing hair color and density and how this may impact the tattoo if you're working on the eyebrows.

- **Number 3**- Access, the Fitzpatrick skin type and undertone. Are you correcting an existing tattoo or working on virgin skin? Use your color wheel to determine if a warm, cool or neutral skill is needed. The color identification chart will indicate the dominant hue.

Remember that:

Pigment + skin tone + healing, overtime = final tattoo result after exfoliation.

- **Number 4** - When mixing, limit yourself to two pigments and one modifier to avoid a muddy or grey-healed outcome. Excessive colorants can reduce saturation and affect aging, as each color's lightfastness varies and may not lighten over time.

- **Number 5** - When combining colors, add the lightest color first and the darkest. You will end up using more pigments otherwise. A modifier can be added to any point if used.

- **Number 6** - Always write down your pigment formula and ratio used. This will ensure that you produce consistent results up in the chop or understand what is required during a correction.

Color Correction

- If healed Green = neutralize with Red

- If healed Blue Grey = neutralize with Orange

- If healed Purple = neutralize with Yellow

- If healed Red = neutralize with Green

Best Pigments for Specific Techniques

While most pigment lines can be used across your cosmetic tattooing repertoire, making some adjustments to your mixture based on the technique can enhance the result.

The following recommendations to consider in practice:

Ombre Or Powder Brows

The case with the eyebrow tattoo procedure is making an initial assessment of the client's existing hair in the area (if any) or whether this will impact the healed result.

Make sure you ask the client if they tint or dye their hair. Refer to the skin tones test, Fitzpatrick analysis, on your pigment color identification chart to make an informed mixture choice. Start conservatively with a lighter pigment mixture, as you can always add depth upon touch-up. This makes it much easier to correct with a complementary color if there is an issue.

For a softer powdered eyebrow result, consider using a dilution solution on your pigmentation mixture. Ombre brows will start at a high delusional level, such as a 50% solution-to-pigment ratio, at the bulb of the eyebrow and progressively work on the 100 percent pigment at the tail. When using a machine to tattoo the eyebrow, consider the impact of needle configuration. The smaller the needle, the cooler and the more ash the color may heal, and a warm modifier will need to be added accordingly.

Eyebrow Microblading

The microblading technique cools your pigment quite dramatically. This is due to the lower surface coverage of pigment in the skin via strokes - the smaller the line, the further light must travel to reflect.

It is generally recommended to add warmth to your mixture or pick a pigment with a warm dominant base unless your client has very warm skin tones, of course.

Certain skin types are poor candidates for this technique and will have inferior retention as well as cooler results. Be mindful of thin, aged, and ruddy skin types in this regard.

Microblading can also be a lengthy process, and your pigment may tend to dry out during the appointment. Some pigment lines have a glycerin formula, which is formulated to stay moist for longer, which may be helpful.

Eyeliner

Eyeliner and lash line enhancements are popular treatments as this subtle tattoo can have a big impact on appearance and time savings. Many requests will be for a black liner, although you may get the occasional client with the reference for brown (be careful; a warm brown can make the whites appear yellow and tired) or even blue to green liners. This section will focus on black eyeliner options, and this reflects client demand. In terms of black pigment, PMU artists can choose a mixture from the following origins.

Black Pigment is made from a combination of primary colors. This is generally not recommended as UV exposure and aging over time will result in the tattoo turning blue or showing a blue hue.

Iron oxide black is preferred, and it's not formed from a mixture of other colors. Iron oxide can be derived organically, or it can be produced synthetically – inorganically and with non-magnetic molecules. Clients may require touch-ups every few years using this pigment.

Carbon black is a deep black pigment created through the thermal decomposition of hydrocarbon, resulting in a small particle size. Only very experienced PMU artists should use carbon black as there is a high risk of migration, and it is best used for lash enhancements rather than upper liner for this reason. Clients with very venous eyelids are more susceptible to migration due to increased blood flow in the area, so avoid this subtype. When applied correctly, this pigment can be quite effective and long-lasting without the addition of modifiers.

Ensure that you don't mix iron oxide and carbon black together, as you will need to adjust your techniques. If you are performing a correction for faded liner, consider doing a straight pass on the modifier color followed by your black pigment (layer technique). Be careful to follow the existing tattoo line in this case, and your overshoot will result in an unsightly orange or green line. If the correction is the mild case, then add some modifier to your target color pigment mixture and proceed with your passes.

In terms of skin tone influences when using iron oxide pigment, add an orange modifier to your mixture for clients with blue in their eyelids. If your client has purple or pink-red eyelids, then this may distort the healed color of your liner. Add some green modifier to iron oxide to neutralize the impact of pinkish skin tone. Finally, note that almost all black pigment will heal with a bluish cast within a year unless you add some warmth to it.

Lip Tattoo

"Give a girl the right lipstick, and she can conquer the world."

Due to their muscular composition and thin skin layer, lips have limited color impact compared to other facial areas. They naturally appear cool due to abundant surface blood vessels, requiring warm pigments (especially orange tones) to counteract the blue in the dermis.

Exercise caution when tattooing certain areas or considering clients unsuitable, particularly those with highly pigmented skin types like Fitzpatrick V to VI. Such skin may cool after healing, requiring multiple sessions with little progress, especially for clients with dark lips or mismatched lip colors. Achieving color consistency may be challenging due to inconsistent melanin stimulation from the needle.

If a client is deemed suitable, emphasize the need for multiple sessions to implant pigment effectively. Begin with a warmer color initially and adjust to cooler tones if necessary. Match the shade to the darkest part of the lips for a natural look but avoid the lip canthus due to pigment migration. Note that the vermilion border requires fewer passes than the center for enhancement.

Correction Techniques, Considerations, and Mistakes to Avoid

As a permanent makeup artist, you will often encounter clients with faded or just collar tattoos. These individuals may be looking for a coverage solution or some advice on removal. To assess whether you can tattoo over the existing pigment, some factors to consider are:

The Density of Old Pigment

Suppose a tattoo is too dark or just discolored (blue or red hues are quite common) for tattooing over. Older tattoos usually have lower density as the pigment has metabolized over time. Also, note that a significant degree of fading will occur upon healing, and thus, the original tattoo can become visible again. Ensure that you communicate this risk to the client.

Location of the Tattoo

Most of the assessments you carry out as a cosmetic tattooist involve the face. This area of the body is quite vascular and metabolizes pigment at a higher rate than all the body regions. Tattoo removal here can be quite painful as the skin is delicate and thinner while being closer to the ligaments of the bone. If you choose to correct rather than refer a client to laser, determine how many sessions you will require and whether this will overwork or stress the skin for a potentially shorter-term outcome.

How Long-Ago the Producers of Our Dogs Were Taken

If it is a recent case where the client is not happy with the result, then you may advise them to try an at-home solution. Using retinol or hydroxyl acids or scrubbing with manual exfoliants can help to promote fading. Suppose the tattoo is a few years old. In that case, you can be confident that any residual pigment is stable and will not change significantly within the next few months. You can make a removal assessment based on what you observe.

If an existing tattoo is too dense to correct, a client can consider the following options:

Dermabrasion – a somewhat dated method that manually removes the skin layers using a sanding device. The higher risk of scarring and skin trauma associated with dermabrasion led the way for less invasive measures like lasers.

Laser Hair Removal – a machine-based procedure undertaken by trained professionals. This method has a high degree of effectiveness if performed right using great-quality lasers. Note that multiple sessions may be required to achieve the desired outcome. For those clients who have been tattooed with a titanium dioxide-based pigment (usually a skin-toned color with whitened appearance), laser is not an option if the tattoo will turn black and oxidize during the treatment.

Saline and Salt Removal or Color Lifting Products

This form of removal can be used for both lighting of old tattoos and corrections for current clients, for example, if you misplace a hair stroke. It Results in the lifting of flaking off pigment via osmosis rather than the breakdown and metabolized removal by the body that occurs during the laser.

PMU artists trained in this technique use a traditional rotary or digital tattoo machine to penetrate the removal solution into the tattoo. The solution is composed of a sterile saline and salt mixture and can either be formulated by a tattooist or purchased in a premixed format (color lifting solution). As with laser hair removal, this method is likely to require more than one session for effective results.

Clients will appear red and scabbed following treatment, and a minimum time frame of eight weeks between treatments will be required to allow for healing. Saline and Salt removal is ideal for people with darker skin tones, sensitive skin, and those who have had an allergic reaction to tattoo pigment. Clients on blood thinning medications are not suitable for this treatment.

Color Correction – Adding a new pigment, which will merge with and counteract the color on the existing tattoo. Tattooists must be well-trained in color theory to undertake this approach. Color correction is much less traumatic than color remover. It is a quick deposit of color with a larger needle configuration that keeps the skin in a much more receptive state than skin that has been through removal. Suppose PMU artists are concerned about what pigment components were used in the original tattoo. In that case, correction is not recommended, as there is a risk of poor reactions with any new attempts at coverage.

Camouflage – a cover up method which is often used by poorly skilled PMU artists. This is not a method of removal or a technique that should be adopted. Be wary of any trainers who endorse this as a feasible practice to avoid at all costs. Tattooing a flesh-toned (titanium dioxide) pigment over an existing tattoo will only temporarily mask mistakes, exacerbating the problem further as removal will be more difficult. Correction of color in permanent makeup requires as much refined pigment application as camouflage.

Additional Considerations

If you will be performing removals in any capacity, protect yourself by signing up with insurers where this is stimulated in the cover terms. Many policies fail to factor in this treatment under the framework of cosmetic tattooing.

Also, be aware of the exceptions for new clients. Remember that cosmetic tattoos implanted into the dermis are intended to be permanent. Removals are a stressful and long process that can take a toll on both parties. Ensure that there is clear communication about the number of treatments required as well as likely results. When In doubt, it is better to refer clients to more specialized parties.

Client Factors

As a well-trained technician, you may have the perfect pigment mixture along with solid technique, but the client is still voicing concerns and complaints about the outcome. This is inevitable in a PMU artist's career, and it can really batter your confidence.

Knowing how to manage these scenarios is critical in reducing stress for you and the client. You must determine the cause of the issue. Consider the following explanations when faced with tattoo color problems and the possible root cause:

• Variability In Client's Color Perception

Color blindness is a lot more prevalent than you might think, although it is more common in males. This can cause clients to report seeing an orange or another hue in their tattoo despite there being no trace on it.

• Misleading Lighting

If a client complains about color, then ask them what light conditions were present in their tattoo. When outside, a tattoo can appear cooler and darker, whereas natural light will generally reduce the appearance of green or blue tones. Ask the client to step outside and inspect again if this is a concern. Tattoos viewed under fluorescent lighting can also present them as quite cool.

- ## Impact Of Makeup

Clients may have concealed their tattoo color by masking them with makeup. Some foundations contain titanium dioxide, and this can cause tattoos to appear grey. Ask the client to wipe their makeup off and reassess before attempting to correct it.

- ## Eye Strain

A client may view their tattoo color inaccurately due to eye strain over a prolonged treatment time. Ensure you have the right lighting conditions in your studio to control this. Clients with lighter irises have a lower tolerance for bright lights – they have lower levels of pigment in their eyes and can experience more discomfort. Dentist lights or quality tattoo equipment brands don't hurt clients' eyes when closed.

- ## Environmental Factors

Clients who spend a lot of time in the sun will find their tattoo color will fade or break down very quickly. To counter this, make sure you empathize with the importance of covering yourself up with sunscreen and hats as appropriate in your aftercare forms.

- ## Skin Care

Excessive cleansing or exfoliating of skin can cause the color of the tattoo to fade or impact retention. Ensure the client avoids using retinoids and harsh acids near the treatment area, as products can spread.

- ## Psychological Factors

You will occasionally have clients who have body dysmorphic disorder (BDD). In the beauty industry, clients with BBB can be common due to preoccupation with the way they look and a tendency to actively seek treatment solutions. People with this mental illness are more likely to perceive defects or flaws in their appearance and constantly worry. They may view a flaw as significant, whereas the general population sees the issue as either minor or not observable. Use your intuition to assess whether a potential client will react negatively to your tattoo. Common Red Flags include excessive scrutiny of all aspects of the treatment – often prior to the appointment (some questions and concerns are normal and expected), frequently asking to check progress in a mirror, and much longer than usual drawing time required. If you do feel that a potential client's expectations are unreasonable, then kindly advise them that you are not a good fit. It isn't worth taking on Business that will only cause stress and lead you to lose confidence.

- ## Key Mistakes to Avoid

While many dependencies can impact the healing result of a tattoo, some repeat color mistakes are often made by new PMU artists. It can be frustrating trying to determine why things aren't working and whether this is down to technique or pigment. Keep the following in mind to minimize risks.

- ## Not Mixing Pigments Properly

This seems overly simple, and it is, but you would be surprised as to how often this is the cause of poor color outcomes. On the physical level, the components of a big pigment will separate in storage. Tattooists must shake the bottle until they are certain that the solution is evenly dispersed before use.

When combining pigment colors or adding modifiers, it is even more crucial that each element is well blended. Some cosmetic tattoos are small plastic caps or pigment rings to formulate their base colors. While this is handy and reduces pigment waste, the small size of these compartments can limit a technician's ability to thoroughly mix their solution.

A toothpick or micro-swab should be used for at least 20 seconds to ensure even distribution. Better yet, use a mini-battery-operated mixer to do the work for you in less time. Note that with lengthier treatments such as microblading, tattooists will often add pigments or rewetting solution to their caps or rings gradually to keep the mixture from dying out. This leads to a risk of having uneven ratios of pigment components over time as colors are added to the old mixture.

• Use Dated or Damaged Supplies

Each pigment bottle will have a use-by date, which you should monitor closely. The distributor will also provide storage instructions and a disposal time frame after each bottle has been opened (usually three to six months, depending on the brand). For whatever reason, perhaps due to the poor tracking of open dates or having an unorganized work set-up, some technicians will only dispose of a pigment after it is completely emptied, which could be years for some unpopular colors! While this may be handy for environmental and economic reasons, using dated supplies can be risky.

Once a pigment is exposed to air after opening, the compounds will gradually oxidize or degrade in quality over time. A previously deep brown hue may not be as potent and impact the healed color. There is also a risk of cross-contamination or bacterial growth in your pigment if a bottle is in high use. Cut your losses and stick to good rotational principles.

• Using Cheaper Brands or Replicas

When preparing your treatment station, you can certainly cut costs by using more affordable supplies. With items such as swabs, disposable aprons or masks and cotton wipes, there is generally a negligible difference between generic store–label and pricier brands. In the PMU field, however, the cost of a pigment line is often reflective of the quality of ingredients and depth of lab testing and research. There are also plenty of fake pigments on the market that claim to be originals of reputable brands. Watch out for these for sale on eBay, Alibaba and Craigslist. A cheaper brand can range from $10 a bottle, while the highly regarded options can be upwards of $60 to $150 each. Ensure that you buy your tattoo ink from a reputable and authorized seller for assurance that you are using poorer-quality products. Don't be tempted by the frugal path.

Using poorer quality pigments will impact your client's tattoo in terms of healed outcome (colors may change, show little implantation, or fade quicker) or even cause an adverse reaction from one of the ingredients.

You don't want the reputation of your business to be affected by the choice of brand. Cosmetic tattooing is a highly referral-based career, and one bad client can make or break your business's longevity. Instead, adjust your treatment pricing to compensate for the cost of your tools of the trade.

- ## Mistaking Color Anomalies and Needle Configuration

  It will take a bit of trial and error, but you will need to master your pigment line. One common mistake during this process is to attribute a poorly healed result to the pigment mixture. For example, a client may return to their top-up treatment with a healed grey or ashy cool eyebrow. While the cause of this outcome was due to the cosmetic tattooist's technique (such as excessive pressure and going too deep into the dermis or using a needle configuration that was too small), they may wrongly attribute this to the pigment that was originally used. Small needles are more prone to slipping through the skin and penetrating too far. This means that the implanted color is located further away from the surface and reflects less light to appear cooler.

If you are using a smaller needle, such as a 1, then add some warm modifier as insurance in your pigment mixture to compensate. It takes time and thought to understand the intricacies of a good tattoo. This will improve throughout your career as you experiment with different skin types.

• Type of Tattoo Equipment

In addition to the impact of needle configurations, the type of tattooing equipment used can also affect the healed color. Newer high-precision digital machines have the functionality to select specific depths. This provides greater reassurance that pigment is being implanted into the correct target area of the dermis. Any unexpected color anomalies are more confidently attributed to the pigment mixture in these cases. In contrast, low-precision equipment such as rotary machines tend to implant pigment at varying depths within the skin and rely heavily on practitioner control. Rotary machines may also penetrate the skin at an angle via sideways oscillations. This can cause tears in the skin, increase the risk of pigment migration, and compound the impact of varying depth. Ensure that you pick your tools of the trade wisely in consideration of your color theory knowledge and experience.

• Adding Too Many Colors

When formulating a range, pigment brands do not aim to create a bottle for every possible hue and shade. Most brands develop a concise toolkit of colors that you can manipulate to achieve your desired shade. This enables you to gain confidence over time by using the same colors again and again, gradually learning how to master them after seeing healed results.

Given this, technicians must combine pigments to form a hue. This is where inexperienced tattooists can run into problems. In the adding and adjustments process, a technician may combine too many pigments to get rid of shade. When you mix too many colors, this reduces the saturation of the original pigment mixture. It also impacts the usually predictable way in which a tattoo will age.

For example, one color may fade more quickly over time, so you will be unsure of what residual or dominant shade the client will be left with. This is because mixing too many colors together change the lightfastness rating of each component.

Stick to no more than two pigments and one modifier if required to avoid a messy result.

Bonus

EYEBROW ANATOMY

"If you don't have brows, you don't really have a face."

Saoire Rehan

Shaping is the process of mapping out your client's eyebrows and drawing them with a pencil to create a pre-draw. Before the pre-draw, you want to take into consideration several factors when it comes to shaping your client's eyebrows. These factors, along with facial asymmetry, are what make shaping the hardest step when it comes to doing brows.

Factors to consider.

- Asymmetry
- Previous Brows Work
- Face Shape
- Hair Growth Imbalance
- Brow/Bone Structure
- Brow Muscle Imbalance
- Amount of Existing Brow Hair

Eye Axis Imbalance

How much brow hair the client has, how thick the individual hairs are, and the existing shape plays a huge role in deciding the shape. Clients with thin and fine brow hairs allow for more flexible shaping. Because each brow hair is thin, blending is much easier if the decided shape is different or thicker than her existing brows. If the client has thick and coarse brow hairs, you ideally want to stay within her existing shape and thickness. If there is a lot of natural brow hair growth outside of the tattooed shape, the client will have to be on top of brow grooming.

Hair growth imbalance can be a major factor to consider when it comes to shaping. If your client has one brow that is higher and one that is lower, compromises will have to be made. You will have to make the higher brow lower and the lower brow higher to meet in the middle and create symmetry. Some brow hairs might need to be sacrificed to achieve even brows in this case.

Face Shape

"You Must Never Underestimate the power of the Eyebrow."

Jack Black

Long

Your client has a long face shape when the width of her face is narrow, and she has elongated features. You want to aim to make the long face shape appear shorter by avoiding high arches and long eyebrows. Their shapes will create the illusion of an even longer face. Straight and flat eyebrows can be ideal since these shapes make the face look shorter.

Heart

Your client has a heart face shape when she has a pointy chin and a prominent forehead. You want to aim to balance the prominent forehead and pointed chin by giving the client a soft and rounded arch.

Diamond

Your client's cheekbones will be the widest part of their face and sit nice and high. The forehead won't be as wide as a heart-shaped face. A diamond face shape requires haircuts, styles and makeup that will bring out the best in narrow and full features that combine to create its unique shape.

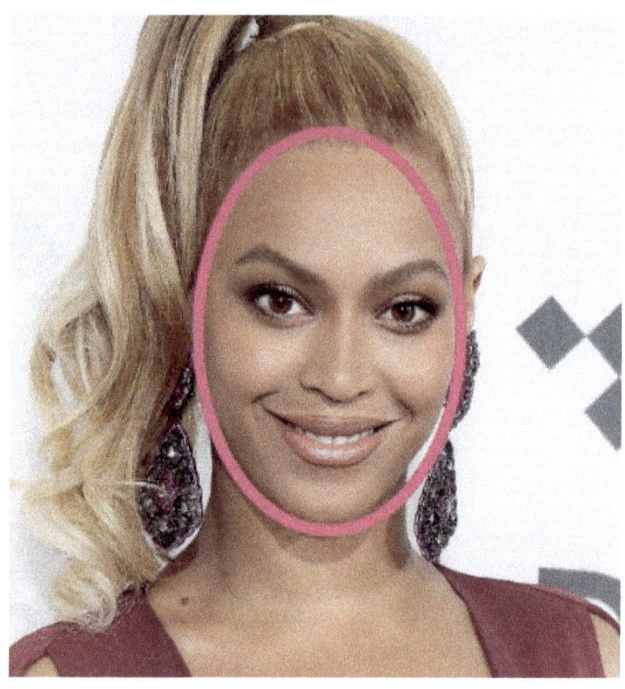

Oval

Your client has an oval face shape when her face is slightly longer than it is wide. The cheekbones will continue be the widest and most prominent part of the face, and the forehead and sides of the face will be slightly curved. For a client with an oval shape, there are generally many eyebrow shapes that will suit.

You should aim to maintain the client's natural face shape.

Square

Your client has a square face shape when her forehead, cheekbones and jaw have the same width. Your client will typically have a prominent jawline. Ideally, you should aim to balance the defined jawline by creating a more defined arch.

Round

Your client has a round face shape when the length of her/ his face is like the width of the client's face. The cheekbones are the widest part of the face, and the chin will be typically rounded. A round face is like a square-shaped face with softer angles. Avoid eyebrow shapes that are too round because round arches will make the face look even more round. A higher arch can break the roundness.

PREVIOUS BROW WORK

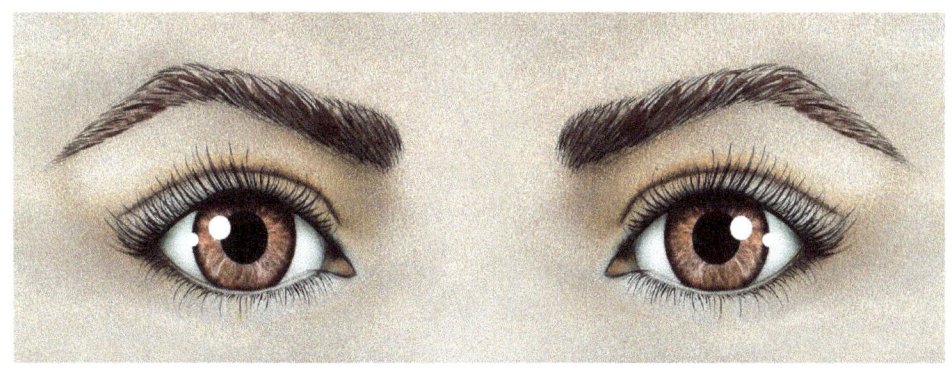

Suppose your client has had previous brow work such as Microblading, Micro shading, Ombre Powder Browns etc. In that case, this will be a major factor to consider when shaping your client. The new shape given must cover your client's previous work. To completely cover the old work, you can expect that the new set of eyebrows will at least be slightly thicker than the original thickness. If there is an asymmetry in the previous work, it will be difficult to achieve symmetry, sometimes even impossible.

The more asymmetrical the previous work is, the thicker the new shape must typically be to achieve symmetry. You will be limited in how you can shape your client since you will be working around the previous artist's work. It is especially important to manage the client's expectations when they have previous brow work. This is why you must screen clients for correction eyebrows or color correction eyebrows because not all sets of eyebrows can be fixed. Sometimes, you would need to use Laser treatment & eyebrow removal treatment to fix the previous work & start a new one.

Space Between Eyebrows are very important as well, for example:

- Bringing the brows too close together will create an "intense" look.

- Bringing the brows too close together may help balance a wide-set eye.

- Bringing the brows closer together may help a close-set eye seem less close.

You and your client must come to an agreement on which brow design you will be creating for your client during the consultation appointment for two main reasons:

1. Your client has time to think about the shape/design and has the opportunity to make changes if they want.

2. In case you both cannot agree on the design, and you decide not to provide the service for that client (You might not want to risk your reputation by doing a job you do not want your name on it)

Mapping the brows

It is recommended that you ask your client to bring pictures of the eyebrow shape/ design they like. Drawing them while using makeup is also a good idea. That way the client gets to see what it really looks like having those brows on them.

The purpose of the pre-draw is to show your client what the eyebrows will look like and get their approval before tattooing. The goal of shaping/ mapping is to enhance your client's facial features while making them as symmetrical as possible. Everyone's face is asymmetrical in one way or another; no one is perfect, and the goal of shaping and brow mapping is to create the illusion of symmetry.

When drawing and mapping an eyebrow, stand back, take your time, and use your artistic eye. Some artists measure while the client is sitting, others while the client is lying down. Consider the shape of the face, including the natural bone structure. Determine where the eyebrows would flow nicely.

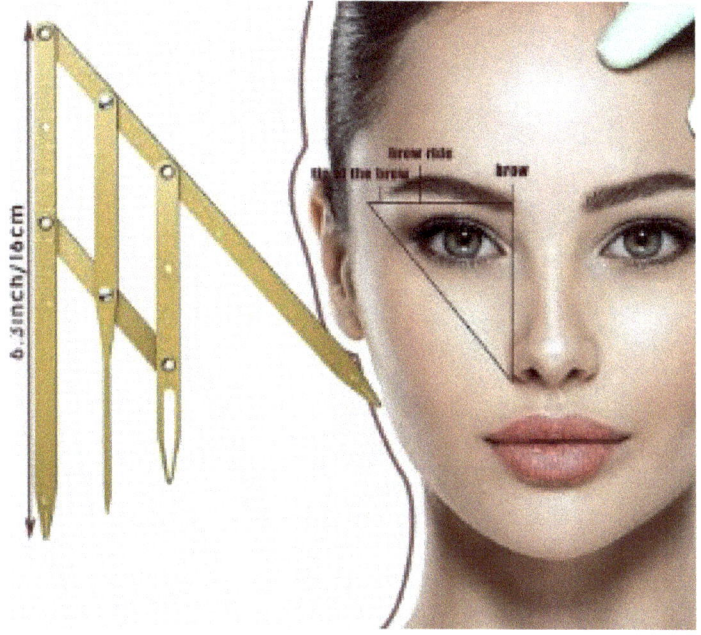

The 3-point caliper uses three measuring points you can duplicate by moving the tool to the other brow.

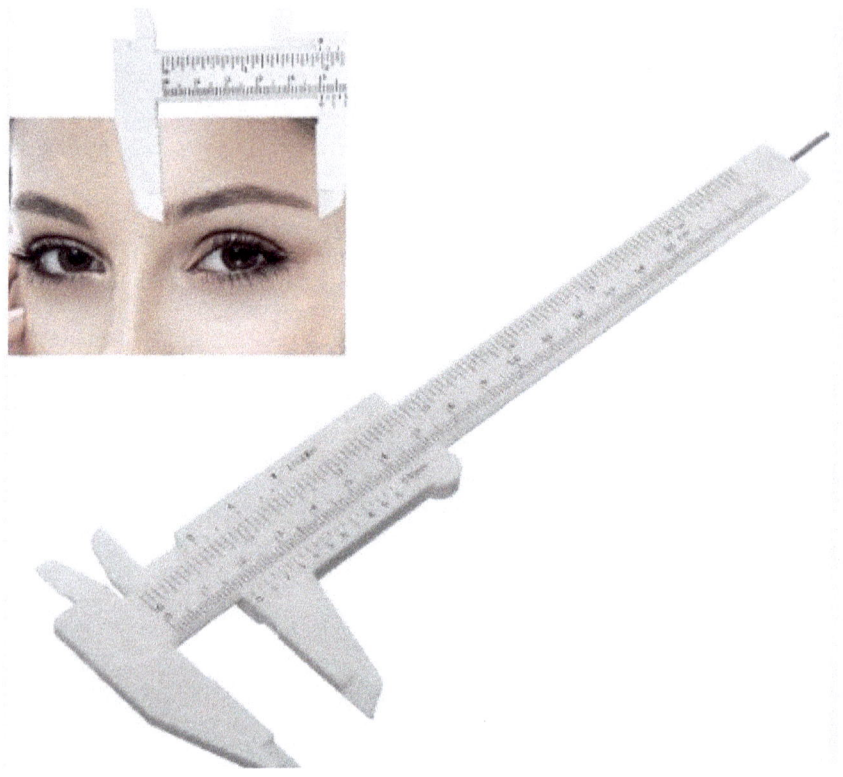

The caliper has 2 moving manual tension arms to measure the distance between different points of the eyebrows.

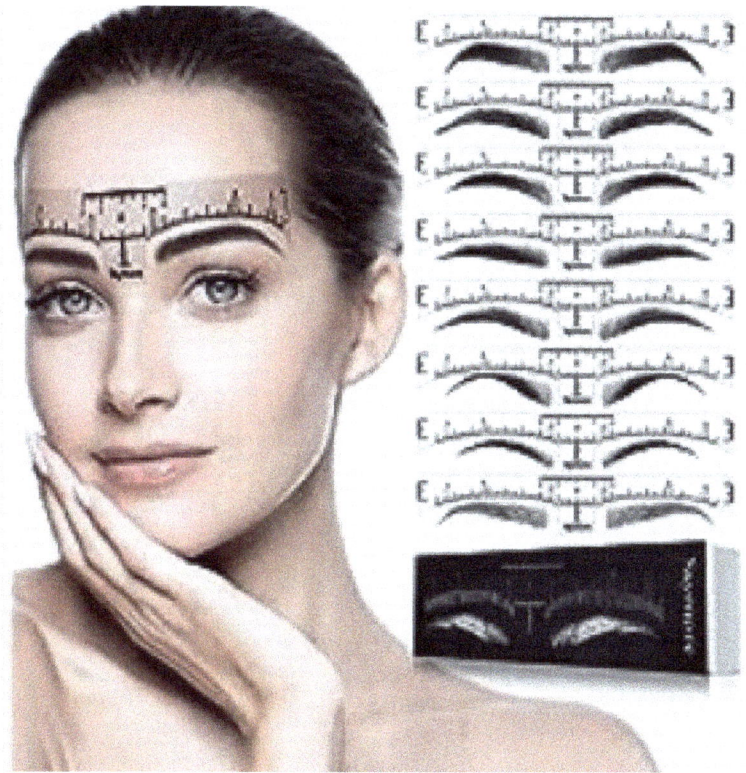

There disposable sticker rulers are available that you can use right on the forehead to mark and measure the eyebrows for symmetry.

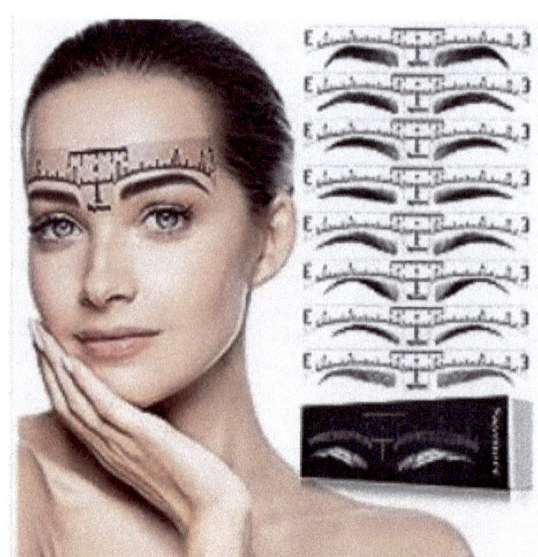

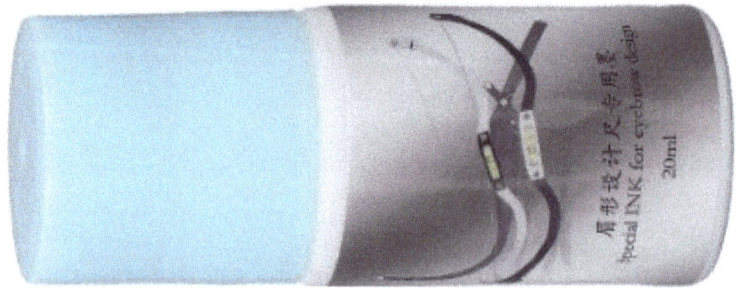

Ink string allows you to draw straight lines more easily.

Step-by-Step Mapping Method

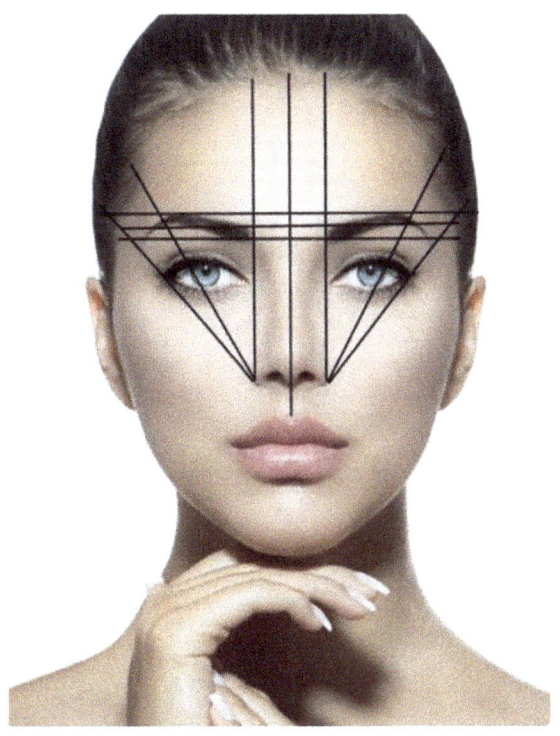

Step 1 – Measure from the outside corner of the nostril, bringing the line up to the crown of the eyebrow.

Step 2 – To find where the natural arch flows, measure straight up from the outside of Iris. On a person with a higher forehead, the arch can be more enhanced. For a person with a lower hairline, a softer arch looks more natural.

Step 3 – Begin to measure the end of the eyebrow tail from the outside corner of the nose and eye, following through towards the temple. Women who want a softer look may request shorter eyebrows.

Step 4 – Measure the center of both eyebrows by placing a line from the middle of the cupid's bow on the lips, straight up along the middle of the nose, to the midpoint of both eyebrows.

Step 5 – Measure across the top of the eyebrows with a straight line, placing it above both arches. This will help achieve the perfect balance needed to ensure symmetrical eyebrows.

Step 6 – Both eyebrows also need to be measured horizontally, across the bottom using a straight measuring tool, measure across at the lowest part of the eyebrows, to ensure perfect balance.

Connecting brow lines

Step 1 – Top Line: Corner of the middle part to the corner arch.

Step 2 – Bottom line: Lines must be parallel, bottom line must be longer.

Step 3 – Top tail: The line can be straight or curved outside.

Step 4 – Bottom Tail: The line should be curved inside.

Pre-Draw

1. Using your brow pencil, round out the top of the arch and the bottom of the arch.

2. Fill in the brow Shape using your brow pencil. Keep the front of the brow light to mimic the from ombre. Blend the pre-draw using Q-Tip if needed. Repeat with other eyebrows.

3. Set aside a portion of concealer using a disposable applicator (Q-Tip, lip wand, etc.) onto the back of your hand (on your glove). This is to avoid constantly dipping your concealer brush into a concealer part and cross-contaminating.

4. With your concealer and concealer brush, conceal the pre-draw. Using the tip of your concealer brush, use small and steady motions to ensure straight and defined lines.

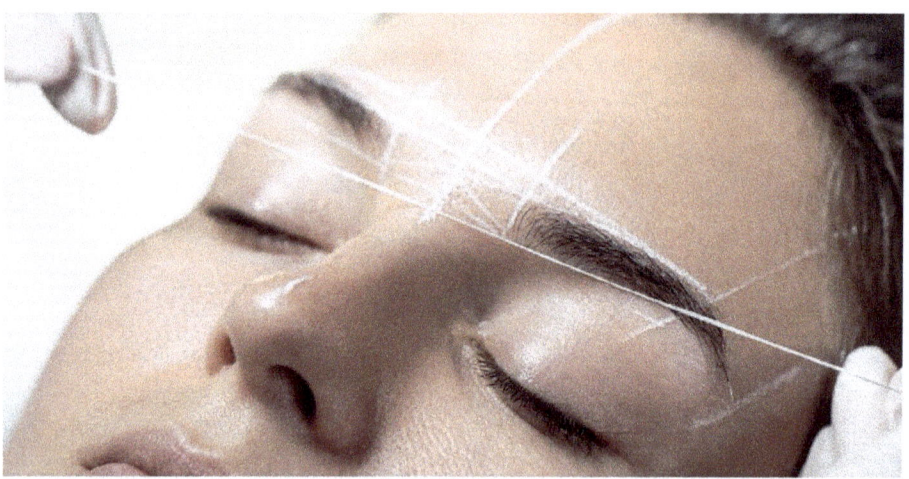

Technique

There are many elements you must take into consideration: choosing the right needle or microblading blade, proper skin stretch, correct angle, and pressure depth.

Stretching

Hands-down, the most important factor in getting great strokes is making great stretches. The key to getting a proper stretch is to flatten the skin in 3 opposing directions. This is called a 3-point stretch. The stretching hand (the hand without the tool) should be placed strategically along the client's forehead to pin the skin down and spread it apart in small, taut stretches. This forms 2 of 3 points. Now, at the same time, the pinky of the working hand must stretch in an opposing direction to complete the 3-point stretch. Just when you think you can't get the skin any flatter, you're almost there. Remember, when the skin is flat, the stroke will be clean since the surface is void of wrinkles and bounces.

3-point stretch:

To do a 3-point stretch, you will do a 2-point stretch with your stretching hand and with the pinky of your machine hand, you will stretch outwards. Your stretching hand will be stretching in the opposite direction as well.

Depth

Depth is critical because if you go too shallowly, you will only land in the upper dermis, and the color won't stay. If you go too deep, you can cause scarring, and the color will heal too ashy. So, how do you figure out the perfect depth? The truth is, it's very tricky as every client has a different skin thickness and often, the skin will be much thinner at the tail of the brows than the build of the brow. In order for the color to stay, you'll need to microblade to the epidermis, but not further. A tell-tale sign that you've hit the epidermis, or the "perfect spot," is when you see a slight channel in the skin, frequently marked by pinpoint bleeding. But not all skin types of bleed. Sensitive skin will bleed more easily, in which case, you will need to lighten your pressure to prevent more bleeding. Too much bleeding will dilute the color. The proper depth often relates to the thickness of the client's skin.

How to tell if your needle is too long – If you're tattooing and no pigment comes out (and you have adequately dipped your needle into the pigment)

And you see is blood. Your needle might be too long.

How to tell if your needle is too short – If you are tattooing and excessive amounts of pigment begin to pour out your needle might be too short.

Outline – For outlining, you should keep your machine straight and upright by holding it at 90 degrees from the skin.

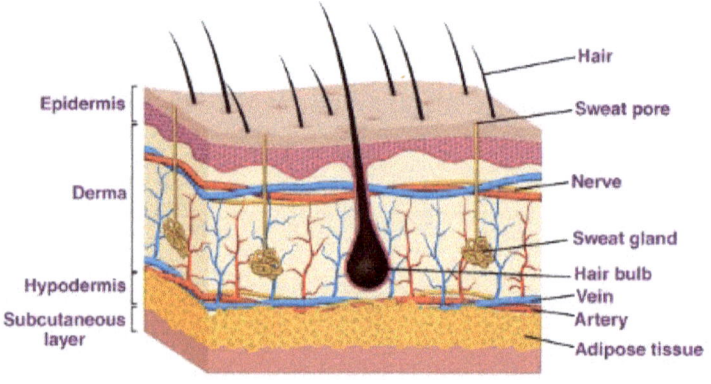

Placement and angle

When implanting color, it's important to have the proper angle and placement of the microblade. The following is the correct way to hold and angel a microblade tool:

- A microblade tool should be held like a pen at a 90-degree angle, as seen in the picture on the following page.

- The handle should be in an upright position, not leaning from the left to the right. If the needles lean in either direction, it cause the hair stroke color to heal blurred.

- Each needled placement must make the same full contact on flat, stretched skin.

- The needle length can be adjusted using the machine. The needle length for tattooing ombre powder brows should be 2.0-2.5mm, and only approximately 1/5 of the needle should enter the skin.

- Although the machine has numerical adjustments that are meant to represent the needle length in mm (millimeters), we don't want to rely on the measurement on the machine. We always want to use our eyes to check the needle length.

- To adjust the needle, twist the knob on the machine.

Skin & Consistency

In microblading, slow always wins. It's very important to use a slow, steady and consistent pace. Not only should you concentrate on making each stroke slowly, but you should also be acutely aware of the place of the entire procedure. Don't get caught up in a speed trap, and accelerate your work as you progress, as your results will suffer. With each case, you will encounter challenges like bleeding, lax skin, or thick patches of hair, and the best way to deal with these challenges is to work at a slow, consistent pace. When you stroke slowly, you will work with more precision and overcome these types of obstacles.

Focus on making each stroke count. Remember, slow and steady wins the race.

Skin comes in 4 thickness varieties: super-thin, thin, regular and thick. You need to understand the tolerance level of the skin to understand its breaking point. Often, the skin will be thinner at the tail of the brow and thicker at the build, so the pressure needs to be adjusted as you work. The thickness of every client's skin is very different. Because of this, you always want to begin with lighter pressure/ less needle depth when tattooing. Start with less needle depth, check if the pigment is too light, and gradually increase pressure. Once the skin begins taking the pigment, remain at that needle depth. Do not increase to speed up the tattoo process. Excessive needle depth may lead to the eyebrows healing too cool or overworked skin. Overworked skin will lead to poor retention after the healing process.

Older skin is thinner than younger skin, so with older clients, you will need to adjust the pressure. Wear a headlamp to really gauge the depths of the cuts you are making.

Knowing the skin and microblade to the tolerance level of that part of the skin will help you microblade to the proper level without overworking the skin, giving you better results.

NEEDLES

There are flexible blades (called "flexi" blades) and hard blades. Needle configurations come in 7-21 pins. The flexi blades are wrapped in a plastic base. White for the regular blades and blue or black plastic base for the Nano blades. Flexi blades are good for beginners, which doesn't mean they're only for beginners. The Flexi is also a good blade to use on anyone from thin or aged skin to regular skin types.

The flexible base helps prevent going too deep as the base absorbs some of the pressure but not all. It is still possible to go too deep with a flexi blade, but not as easily as with a hard blade. The positive to using a flexi blade is the safety net it provides. The con is that it is not as steady as the hard blades.

The hard blade's base is aluminum (silver or gold) and is unforgiving. The hard blades are very stable but have no give. It is a good blade to use on regular to thick skin, although not recommended for thin or sensitive skin. Hard blade com in needle configurations from 7-21 pins.

Needle Rows

The Fewer needles present, the thinner the strokes will be. And the smaller the needle configuration used for the eyebrow procedure, the more ash (ash is always cooler (green/blue) and darker) the healed procedure will appear. Why? Because the smaller needles slice through the skin more effectively and generally place pigment deeper. The use of larger needle configurations has less of a slicing effect and, for Lack of a better word, plummets pigment into the skin, thus placing the pigment slightly closer to light and further from a direct relationship with the bloodstream (blue). The pigment that remains closer to the surface of the skin will reflect lighter and appear less cool than the pigment that recedes deeper in the skin.

Blades

Below are the most used needles/ blades. Perfect for beginners and advanced professionals.

7-pin blade:

the single row 7-pin blade is your finest of all the blades. This blade will be good for creating shorter, thinner hairs. It is a good blade for thin brows and for little in-between hairs. Good for detailed work. This little guy is designed to give high-definition fine hair strokes. It is ideal if you want to target two existing hair strokes with accuracy- for example, if you want to add a different color. It is suitable for all skin types.

12-pin blade:

Used to create medium-length eyebrow hairs of medium thickness. This is the blade most often used. It is a multi-purpose needle, which is a great starter needle for students because it gives fine lines. It is ideal for blonde women with natural hair, as it can emulate them accurately.

Because it is flexible, it doesn't go too deep, so it is ideal for beginners as you avoid color migration. It also gives you the option to repeat the hair stroke with less pressure for a more defined result.

14-pin blade:

used to create long eyebrow hairs of medium to above medium thickness. This blade is good for creating thicker brows.

U-shape blade:

The 'U" shape blade is great for the inner corner of the eyebrows. As in the inner corner, for great results, you need to be able to draw smooth, angled curves in a short space.

18 super fine single needles:

good for drawing curvy hairs and recommended for the more experienced technician. It allows you to create truly stunning results and superfine lines if you know how to use it. Because there is no gap between the needles (18 to 21 super fine needles are packed into a small surface area with no gap).

Blade thickness

Blades come in different diameters or thicknesses. The thickest blade and one artist rarely use anymore, is the *.35mm* (not recommended)

.25mm – thick skin – great for creating thicker hair strokes.

.22mm- average skin

.20mm- average skin

.18mm (nano) – thin skin. Great for very thin in-between strokes

.15mm – (nano – NOT RECCOMENDED)

Blade Angle

Flexi angled blade is the best blade for beginners. All the needles touch the skin at the same time, making it easier to control the depth in which we are microblading. It is important to master this blade before moving on to the angled blade.

Curved blade – good for making curved strokes, but the mid-section can cause trauma to the skin in the less experienced artist. With this blade, all the needles never hit the skin at the same time. Curved blades are good for making curved strokes.

Creating STROKES

The microblading strokes are what give the brows that 3d hair-like look. To be successful, you must learn the proper techniques to accomplish natural hair-like strokes. Keep in mind that brow hair growth tends to grow in 3 directions: upward, across, and downwards. Study the natural brow and take note of the growth pattern, as you'll need to be able to draw different hair stroke designs to satisfy each client's eyebrow needs.

To create the most natural finish, follow the "3 section rule. "

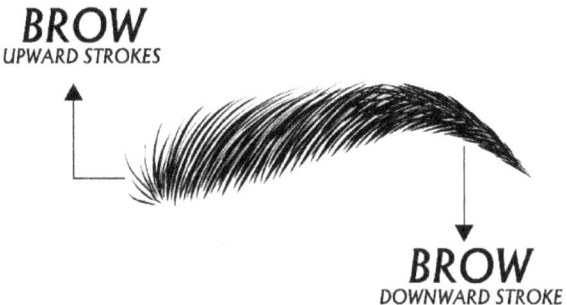

BROW
UPWARD STROKES

BROW
DOWNWARD STROKE

- FRONT SECTION OF BROW UPWARD STROKES

- MIDDLE SECTION OF BROW UPWARD & ACROSS STROKE

- END SECTION OF BROW DOWNWARD STROKE

To give the most natural finish, aim for soft, smooth curves, with fluidity in pressure applied throughout the stroke. Work nice and slowly and try to space strokes at least 1mm apart to prevent migration of the pigment. Remember that correct pressure and skin type are key to producing the perfect hair stroke.

When drawing strokes, be sure you follow these basic steps/rules.

Strokes should not overlap.

If the front of the brow looks clean and is healing nicely, but the middle and tail of the brows appear patchy, then this is an indicator that you must work on your stroke placement. As with the front, middle and tail parts of the brow, strokes should have their own position and place.

Equal distance between strokes.

Each stroke that I place on my client's brows is a precise distance between them. If you need some guiding assistance when doing this, you can put dots around the shape to assist you with guiding the distance by eye.

Nice curve
Good pressure

Too curved
Blunt ends

Too straight
Blunt end

Curve and pressure.

Drawing unrealistic lines can give an unrealistic look. Each stroke should resemble a hair-like stroke, thin and tampered. If you are pressing too hard the stroke will be thick and can possibly heal wrong. Light and thin strokes work best.

The length of each stroke should match the thickness of the eyebrow. If the thickness of the eyebrow is 6mm, this will be the approximate length of the stroke. Strokes in the very front should be shorter.

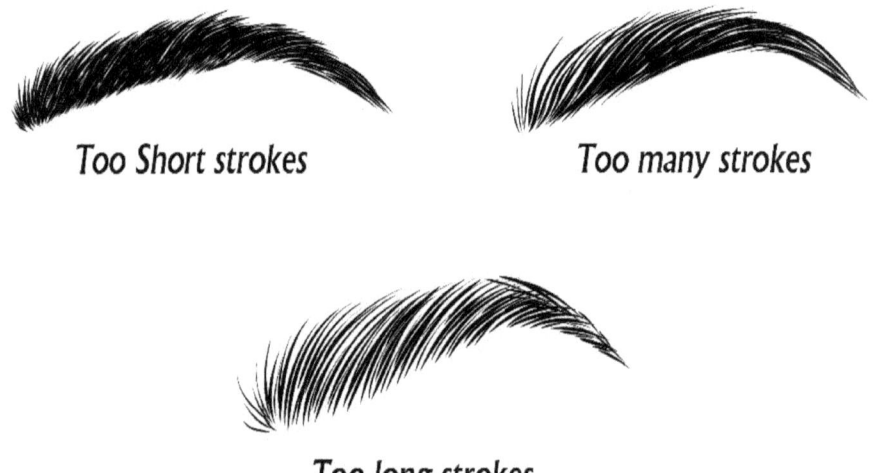

Too Short strokes   **Too many strokes**

Too long strokes

Here, you'll learn how to create strokes for each section of the brow. Follow along with each pattern and practice.

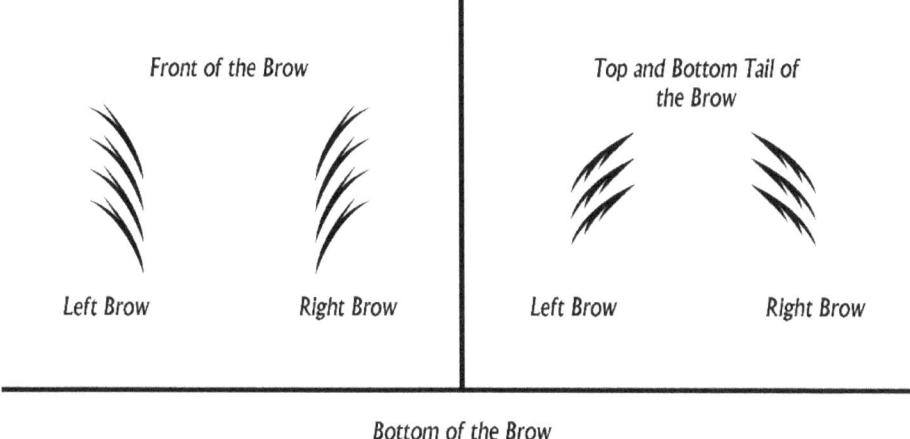

Here, you'll learn how to create connecting and transitioning strokes that connect all strokes. Follow along with each pattern and practice.

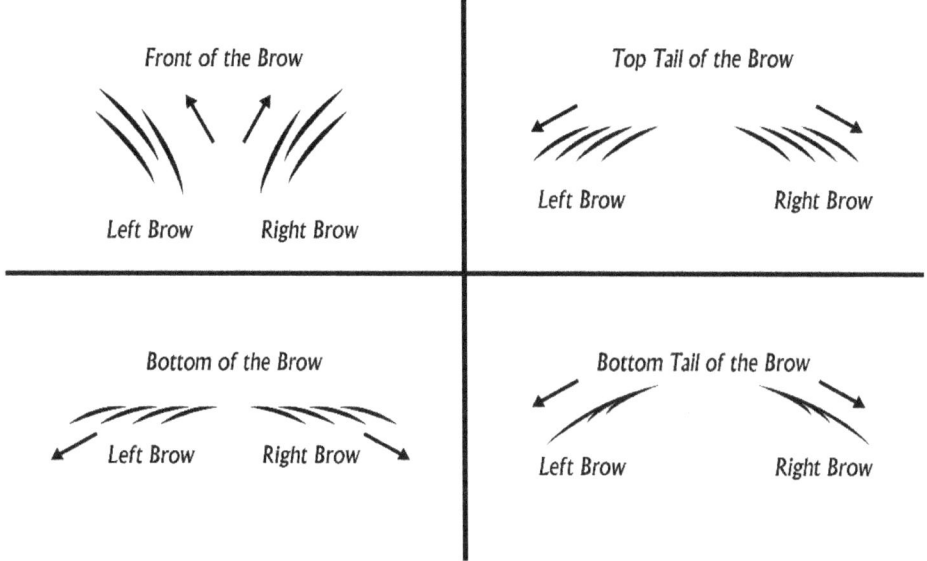

Basic Stroke Pattern

STRAIGHT	
CURVED	
SOFT ARCH	
HIGHT ARCH	
UPWARD	

The basic microblading pattern is designed to mimic the growth of natural eyebrow hairs. There are many different patterns that you can learn but having a basic pattern will help you as a beginner to master the technique. You should be 100 % comfortable and confident with this pattern before performing the procedure on a client.

To make this as simple as possible, we have broken down the pattern into 5 simple steps.

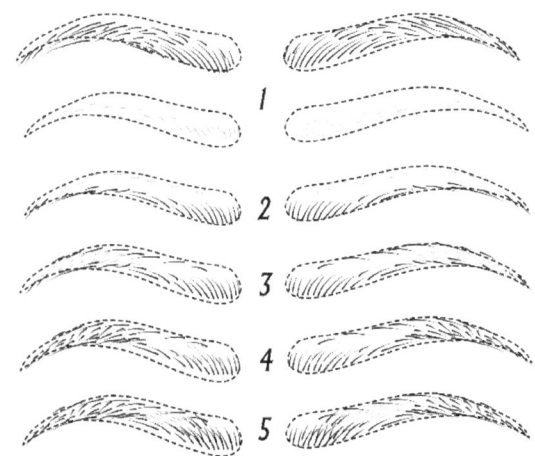

1. Each step is demonstrated in gold. You will need to replicate all the strokes (black and gold) in each example.

2. The dotted outline is provided as guidance when drawing your strokes.

3. Use a sharp pencil for this exercise. Ensure that your pencil is held in a vertical (90 degrees), upright position.

4. Draw the strokes slowly when completing each step.

5. Practice drawing symmetrical brows.

Make a brow contact before eye contact 😉

EYEBROWS ART PRACTICE

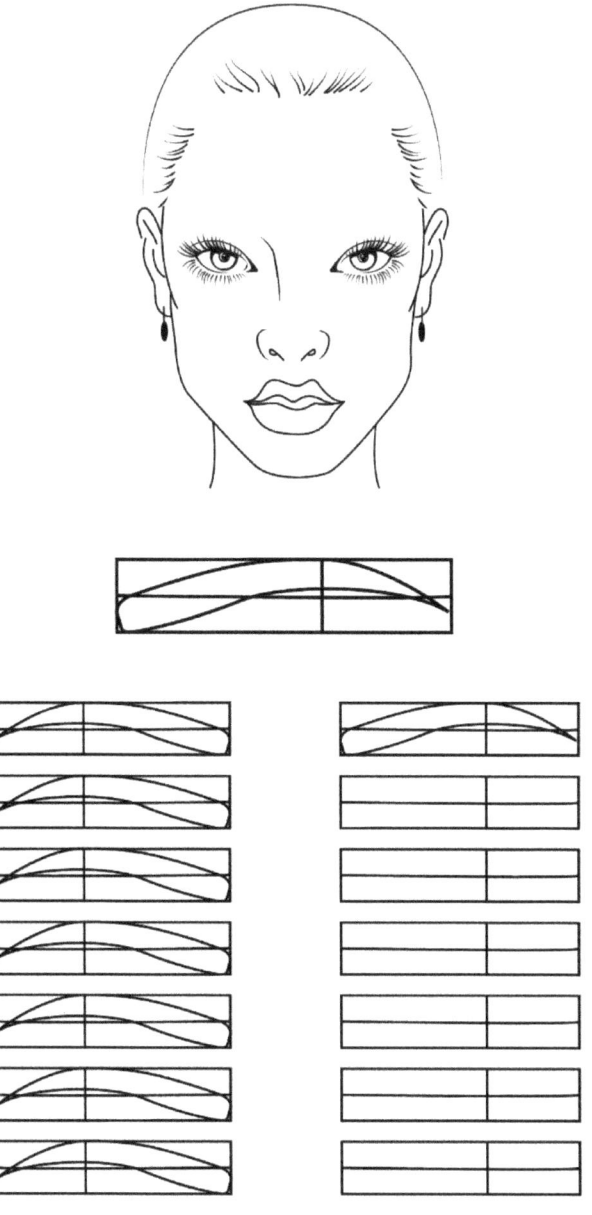

Microblading procedure Step by Step

1. GO OVER CONSENT FORMS WITH A CLIENT

2. PERFORM A THOROUGH CLIENT CONSULTATION

3. TAKE BEFORE PHOTOS

4. NUMB THE BROWS AND COVER WITH PLASTIC WRAP. LET SET FOR 30 MIN. WIPE AWAY WITH ALCOGOL. IF YOU DESIGN/MAP FAST, DO THIS FIRST OR SKIP AND DESIGN/MAP FIRST THEN MAP.

5. SETUP YOUR PROCEDURE TRAY.

6. BEGIN BY MAPPING OUT THE DESIRED BROW SHAPE.

7. USE A SURGICAL MARKER TO DOT THE BROW SHAPE AND THE BROW SPINE.

8. START OUTLINING WITH THE MACHINE.

9. REPEAT 2 TIMES TO MAKE SURE THE OUTLINE IS VISIBLE.

10. ONE BROW AT A TIME. COMPLETE THE HEAD STROKES, UPPER STROKES, LOWER STROKES, AND TRANSITION/CASCADE STROKES.

11. MASK WITH PIGMENT

12. WIPE AWAY THE NUMBING GEL WITH ANTISEPTIC FOAM.

13. REPEAT STEPS 10-12 3-4 TIMES.

14. AFTER THE FINAL PASS, LET PIGMENT AND NUMBING GEL SET FOR 5-10 MIN THEN WIPE AWAY WITH ANTISEPTIC FOAM

15. REVEAL BEAUTIFUL NEW BROWS TO YOUR CLIENT

16. TAKE AFTER PHOTOS AND VIDEOS.

17. APPLY VASELINE OR CREAM BY OUR CHOICE OF SOOTHING CREAM TO THE BROWS.

18. GIVE CLIENT AFTER-CARE INSTRUCTION CARD AND KIT.

19. SET UP 6-8 WEEK APPOINTMENT AND GET A DEPOSIT.

20. BREAKDOWN WORKSTATION AND DISPOSE OF ALL HAZARDOUS WASTE IN THE CORRECT DISPOSAL.

TOUCH UP APPOINTMENT

Touch ups are done about 6-8 weeks from the initial procedure. Some clients are satisfied with their brows after just the first session and prefer not to do the first touch-up but come back annually to maintain the shape and color of their brows/lips. It is imperative for clients who have stubborn and/ or oily skin to get a touch-up the first time and annually (every 6 months). Color will fade significantly within 4 weeks as the skin heals, peels, and fades.

The touch-up should take approximately 1 hour and is usually included in your service. The touch-up corrects any irregularities in the strokes and color tones and finishes the process. Mainly, go over previous strokes or part of a stroke that the ink didn't quite deposit well or the strokes completely disappeared.

The touch-up is an opportunity for the professional to settle any of the progressions that may have happened. Also. Before you ask. Yes. Even changed ink color can be rectified! It's also an opportunity for your permanent makeup artist to roll out any little corrections or changes to the shape. Touch-up procedures require the same aftercare as the original procedure, but the healing process does not take as long.

Conclusion

Grasping the concepts of color theory as it applies to permanent makeup is an ongoing learning process. Without this knowledge, even tattooists with enviable flair at applying eyebrows and pinpoint eyeliners will fail. Those who master both technique and understanding of color have the fundamentals to succeed long-term in this industry.

In this comprehensive guide, seasoned permanent makeup artist Inna Argo shares invaluable insights gained through years of experience in the field. From understanding color theory to perfecting pigment mixing, each chapter is meticulously crafted to empower practitioners with the skills necessary for impeccable client results and a flourishing career in PMU.

"Beauty is not in the face; beauty is a light in the heart."

Khalil Gibran

Keep practicing and applying the concepts in this booklet until you develop a natural intuition for corrections and pigment mixing. This skill set will be invaluable for your client results and your career as a PMU.

The difference between ordinary and extraordinary is practice.

Good luck, and don't be too hard on yourself on your great journey.

www.ingramcontent.com/pod-product-compliance
Lightning Source LLC
Chambersburg PA
CBHW051212120626
46547CB00013B/1323